UNDER THE PINES

The Third Twenty Years

**Northwestern
Michigan
College**

Traverse City, Michigan

Copyright © 2013 Northwestern Michigan College

All rights reserved. No part of this book may be reproduced or transmitted in any form or by any means, electronic or mechanical, including photocopying, recording, or by any information storage and retrieval system, without permission in writing from the publisher.

Reasonable effort has been made by the publisher to credit organizations and individuals with regard to the supply of photographs; however, the source of some photography is unknown.

This book was developed with approval from the Board of Trustees of Northwestern Michigan College.

Published by Northwestern Michigan College
1701 East Front Street
Traverse City, Michigan 49686

ISBN: 978-0-9679632-1-1
Book design by Barbara Hodge • www.barbarahodgegraphicdesigner.com
Project Coordination by Nikki Stahl of Peabody BookWorks

Printed in the United States of America
17   16   15   14   13   •   5   4   3   2   1

To the students, staff, faculty, trustees, and volunteers who continue to make NMC Michigan's longest-running community college success story.

Contents

INTRODUCTION – 1992-2011: From Forty to Sixty 1

OUR COMMUNITY COLLEGE.. 9
   A Time to Build 11
   The Dennos Museum Center..19
   The Great Lakes Campus...29
   Parsons-Stulen Technical Education Center (M-TEC) 41
   Aero Park Laboratories Opens 49

ACADEMIC ACHIEVEMENT.. 51
   From Terms to Semesters..53
   The University Center..59
   Four-Year Degree Partnerships..68
   International Aviation 71
   New Degrees and Credentials 77
   Extended Education...85

STUDENT LIFE 89
    Clubs and Special Interests 90
    East Hall Fire 93
    Parking Progress 95
    A Tobacco-Free Campus 99

MONEY MATTERS 103
    A "Culture of Philanthropy" 105
    Lena Jensen's Gift 108
    Annual Campaign for Scholarships and Programs 111
    The Capital Campaigns 114
    The Commitment Scholarships 116
    NMC Barbecue 121
    Cadillac Campus Closes 124
    The Millages 126
    The 1999 Bond Issue 129
    Economic Impact Study 132

SOFTWARE AND HARDWARE 137
    A Fiber-Optic Backbone 139
    The NMC Website 140
    Online Classes and Registration 141

OF COMETS, VESSELS, AND ONLINE STREAMING ...147
Rogers Observatory 149
The Maritime Academy's Ship Comes In 153
WNMC Reaches New Audiences 155

GOVERNANCE 161
The Board of Trustees Makes a Transition 163
A History of Great Leadership 169
Tim Quinn: 1989-1996 169
Ilse Burke: 1996-2001 171
Tim Nelson: 2001-Present 175

THE FOURTH TWENTY YEARS 179
Global Initiatives 181
NMC, Always Looking Ahead 183

APPENDICES 187
Board of Trustees 187
Presidents 188
Imogene Wise Faculty Excellence Award Recipients 188
Adjunct Faculty Excellence Award Recipients 189
Outstanding Alumni 190
Foundation Excellence Award Winners 191

INTRODUCTION

*1992-2011
From Forty
to Sixty*

Northwestern
Michigan
College

Grand Traverse voters were asked to approve a $34.7 million renovation bond in 1999.

WE'RE ON A FIRST-NAME BASIS; we're trusted friends. That's certainly the relationship implied by those of us who refer to Northwestern Michigan College as, simply, "the college." That feeling of familiarity belies a proud sixty-year history of an educational institution constantly assessing, striving, and changing in service to its larger purpose: community-based learning for everyone.

As a community college, NMC's challenge is to serve all students, from dual enrollees, recent high school graduates, and young adults choosing a new career after real workforce experience to the academically curious, the outsourced, the downsized, or the retiree looking for intellectual renewal. These are just a few of the kinds of learners who make up NMC's student body. They are a vastly diverse population that nonetheless comprises people who all have at least one thing in common: a passion for learning.

Perhaps NMC President Timothy Nelson puts it best: "Our job is to make sure all those learners learn."

This goal of satisfying any and all students' quests for new skills and knowledge has been NMC's ongoing mission ever since it opened its doors in 1951 inside borrowed classrooms with sixty-five students and six teachers. In the ensuing years, NMC has made a financial commitment to making sure all those learners learn. Although NMC is not the largest community college in Michigan, the NMC Foundation awards more scholarship dollars to more students than any other community college in the state.

With four campuses plus an observatory, an FM radio station, a website, a ship, boats, and airplanes, the college has a staggering number of people interacting with it in its sixtieth year: more than five thousand academic students enrolled, more than nine thousand extended-education students, more than three hundred faculty and staff employed to teach them, plus 110,000 stargazers who have visited the Rogers Observatory, half a million hungry diners who have been served by the annual Barbecue, and more than one million visits to the Dennos Museum Center since its doors opened in 1991.

While the college's service area remains officially defined as Grand Traverse, Leelanau, Kalkaska, Antrim, and Benzie counties, in this, its third twenty years, those demarcations have become just geographical lines on a map, no longer defining the boundaries of the college's service area. With many classes now available online; with regional, statewide, national, and even international partnerships secured; and with international students and faculty increasingly selecting northern Michigan as their learning destination, in NMC's sixtieth year, our local community college has truly attained a global reach.

That NMC has been able to successfully grow, develop, and change so dramatically and yet remain relevant to its region in its past twenty, then forty, then sixty years is remarkable. That it has managed to do so in such a spectacular and even aesthetically pleasing fashion while retaining its precious sense of community is exactly what makes it "the college." Our college.

"Quality is a key word," said NMC Fellow and former Trustee Elaine Wood. "That has been the hallmark from day one. A hallmark that has never wavered. NMC has done nothing but go beyond quality, year after year."

In March of 1973, Preston N. Tanis, president emeritus of NMC, wrote *Northwestern Michigan College: The First Twenty Years*, which covered the college's history from 1951 to 1971. Then in February of 1994, Al Shumsky, assisted by Carole Marlatt, wrote *Northwestern Michigan College: The Second Twenty Years*, which covered the college's history from 1971 to 1991. Detailed in these pages is the college's third twenty years, which, even as we recount them, show a community institution focused on the future in its fourth twenty years and beyond.

Consider the photo taken at the Rogers Observatory in 1996, which has the distinct honor of being cataloged in NASA's archives as the official photo of the comet Hyakutake. And consider that an astronaut carried NMC's pennant into outer space and then brought it back to campus. Just like that photograph, and just like that pennant, in its third twenty years, the college has extended its reach without ever losing sight of where it all began: with a community of learners. Never in NMC's history has this been more true than in the years from 1991 to the start of 2012.

Front entrance to the Dennos Museum Center, 1995.

OUR COMMUNITY COLLEGE

Coming into Its Own

Northwestern
Michigan
College

Partial demolition of the "old freezer building" on Front Street, 2001. The building debris was used to raise the elevation of the site.

A Time to Build

TAKE A WALK AROUND the main campus of Northwestern Michigan College today and the architecture of the buildings, the canopy of mature trees, the purposeful sidewalks, the careful maintenance, and the entire mood of the facility all convey learning, study, and what we've come to think of as modern-day academia. But this has not always been a priority conveyed by NMC's physical plant. No, this feeling of heads bent in study, of teachers sharing their knowledge, of students socializing and collaborating, of skill building, is something that the college and its leaders have worked hard to create, especially in the past two decades. It has rarely been an easy task.

Back in 1951, a group of NMC's founders traveled to California and Colorado to get ideas on community college construction. From that trip came eight priorities for the new buildings, among them this one: "Learning can take place in very modest and inexpensive physical settings."

This frugal, no-frills approach was appropriate for its time, but when the college was faced with rapid growth that dictated an equally rapid response, it led to a campus composed, by the 1990s, of functional buildings with little architectural flair and in dire need of long-overdue maintenance.

"We had $5 million or $6 million worth of deferred maintenance," said longtime Trustee Cheryl Gore Follette, who served more than twenty years, starting in 1991. "The board made a commitment that we needed to be better stewards of our assets."

By 1991, the modern-styled Dennos Museum Center had opened to great acclaim, and by 1995, the University Center had opened its doors, too, across town on Boardman Lake south of downtown Traverse City. These buildings were new, state-of-the-art, and pleasing to the eye. They were also the exception. Most of the facilities on the main campus in the 1990s were starting to show their age; when grouped together, they even conveyed an intangible quality that could be described as unwelcoming.

Even the drive in and out was unremarkable. NMC's main entryway, College Drive, threaded past parking lots, boiler houses, and dumpsters. For all its growing relevance to the community it served, the college still lacked an academic atmosphere and something that might be considered small in scope yet essential in meaning: a "front door."

While some argued that an aesthetically pleasing campus wasn't all that important for a community college, as NMC's leaders became savvy about the value of a sense of place in the modern-day competition for students, the desire to make the physical campus more appealing took hold. If students weren't attracted enough to NMC to enroll, the faculty would never get a chance to show what it could do in the classrooms. Plus, rigorous learning demanded that the classroom environment be tailored to its task, with suitable technology, lighting, acoustics, and climate control. By the 1990s, the buildings and classrooms at NMC were not keeping up with the needs of the students they were constructed to serve forty years prior. Learning no longer always involved a teacher at the front of a classroom lecturing to silent students. Learning also took place in small groups, in activity, and in collaboration.

Changes in the look of NMC's main campus began in the fall of 1996 with what the board of trustees labeled the "Front Door Project." Front Street was realigned next to the

Dennos Museum Center, creating a safer, more perpendicular intersection, as well as space for a sculpture garden and eye-catching landscaping to draw people in. Then came the more formal and welcoming entrance to the campus, an invitation to students, the community, and visitors to enter and enjoy. In 1999, voters approved a $34.7 million renovation bond that addressed maintenance and space issues on the main campus, polished up the University Center and added its second floor, and finalized funding for a technical center, too. With that historic yes vote and with the overwhelming support of the northern Michigan community, the real transformation of the college began. More than just a construction project, the buildings would serve the intellectual capital and student learning that NMC always made a high priority.

"It's important to note that faculty and staff were involved in planning what we wanted in terms of the new physical environment," said Stephen Siciliano, vice president for educational services. "The design of the new buildings was driven by the needs of our academic programs. There were faculty field trips all around the state to identify what we wanted for our students, what would best serve them, the college, and the community."

Between 1999 and 2011, the white freezer building on Front Street was demolished, the maintenance department and automotive programs it housed were relocated, the library was renovated, science labs and classrooms were upgraded, and the Parsons-Stulen Technical Education Center became the centerpiece of NMC's new Aero Park Campus. In June of 2000, two signs, artistically crafted out of the same stone as that used to build the Dennos Museum Center, were installed at the new entrance to the main campus. The Great Lakes Campus opened in 2003 and 2004. Renovations transformed the old Science Building into Scholars Hall in 2003, complete with an inviting new light-filled entrance and new classrooms and study spaces. The old Communications Building became Founders Hall, also in 2003, with new conference rooms and a new and modern entryway. Finally, parking and traffic on the main campus were improved, and the University Center was expanded.

As then-President Ilse Burke saw it in 1998, when the bond issue was being planned, the huge building project that was about to begin was exciting for the community because it reflected the learning going on within the college. The new look was a physical manifestation of the community's support of NMC and a tangible reminder that people working together could accomplish great things. As NMC's faculty, staff, and administration worked together on long-deferred building maintenance and on designing and constructing the new facilities, their cooperation and drive showed that they could also work together on the more intangible but equally important issues of governance, policy, and curriculum.

Confirmation of NMC's mission and the community's financial investment in that mission arrived from the outside world in short order. The Dennos Museum Center received a prestigious Governor's Award for Arts and Culture in 2000; Rogers Observatory was selected in 1999 as one of only ten sites nationwide to participate in Project Astro, an innovative educational program; and the college received another ten-year accreditation by the North Central Association of Colleges (NCA).

Today, NMC's physical environment has been transformed—but transformed in such a way that its new and beautiful structures not only are pleasing to look at but also encourage learning and interactivity. Instead of being places where students visit for one or more classes and then go home, the new buildings encourage students to linger. Areas called "student commons" in corners and at the ends of hallways of the newer buildings, furnished with comfortable chairs complete with attached desks for writing or resting a book or a laptop, invite study. Other areas have counters where students can spread out and study together. All enclaves are technology ready, with outlets to plug in laptops, tablet computers, and smartphones and data ports for Internet connections.

The idea behind these student commons is to create environments that will lead to student-instructor interaction, student-student socializing and conversation, and the informal learning that is sure to take place whenever people gather.

No longer do people show up, go to class, and leave. Thanks to good planning, they collaborate, both in and out of the classroom. Lingering is encouraged because it's another way to learn.

Maintaining NMC's physical plant has become a priority for the administration, so students, faculty, and visitors can be assured that NMC will continue to present a place of modern-day academia far into the future.

"We have created an infrastructure that is directed at student learning," said President Tim Nelson.

18 | UNDER THE PINES The Third Twenty Years

Early 1990s photo of the main gallery of the Dennos Museum Center.

The Dennos Museum Center

TRAVERSE CITY'S STADIUM. That was past NMC President Ilse Burke's pet name for the Dennos Museum Center, the planning and initial fundraising for which took place under her leadership. It's an attention-getting metaphor she explains this way: Big universities draw in members of their surrounding communities with football. NMC does it with culture—with art, music, lectures, community cinema, and more. Planning, funding, and building the Dennos Museum also rallied community support for the college as a whole, just when it was needed most.

When the Dennos Museum Center opened in 1991 to community-wide expressions of pride, NMC essentially presented a gift of culture to all of northern Michigan. The controversy that had arisen regarding the college's plans to cut down several mature pine trees to build the museum had been assuaged by planners' willingness to reduce the size of the parking lot in order to save some of the trees. When it officially opened, the Dennos Museum Center was embraced.

"I don't believe we built this place to recycle Traverse City," said Dennos Museum Center Director Eugene Jenneman. "My goal is to infuse the region with cultural opportunities from around the world."

In the past twenty years, a million visitors have been treated to such diverse offerings as Andy Warhol photography, U.S. presidential portraits, bronzes from Asia, and the startling and thought-provoking science exhibit "Bodies Human: Anatomy in Motion," which displayed more than one hundred preserved human specimens. African guitars, Chinese acrobats, Celtic fiddles, and political satire have entertained and enlightened audiences from the Milliken Auditorium stage. Community Cinema, an outreach project of CMU public television and the Dennos Museum Center, has shared independent films with the community for free, bringing audiences a wide variety of stories from across the globe and close to home.

These are just a tiny percentage of the experiences the Dennos Museum Center has made available to students, faculty, and the community, securing NMC's reputation as not only a cultural destination but also an educational institution with a history of delivering on its promises when it comes to planning, financing, and completing major projects.

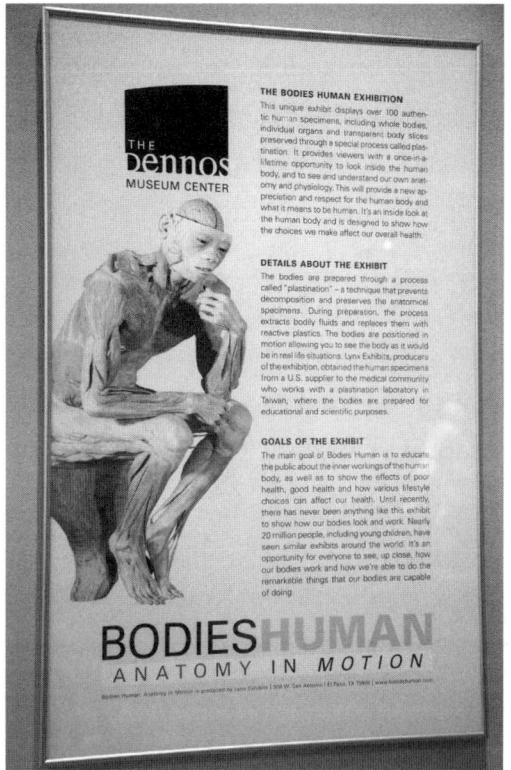

Advertising poster for the Bodies Human *exhibit at the Dennos Museum Center, 2011.*

Kathleen Guy, vice president for institutional advancement and executive director of the NMC Foundation, said that successfully opening the Dennos Museum Center was the turning point for NMC's credibility with the community, with philanthropic donors, and with the state government.

"Once our ideas matured for the museum center and as we were able to take those ideas to the broader community, people began to get as excited about NMC as we were," she said. "The Dennos was our first capital campaign, and we were building our fundraising muscles. What we discovered was that people would make philanthropic gifts to the college."

Jenneman said that even before it opened, he had hopes that the museum would help turn NMC into a complete learning environment. That hope continues to be realized with each new exhibit, with each concert, and in each large audience for the college's International Affairs Forum.

"I've always felt that the role of the museum should be to give the region opportunities it wouldn't have any other way," Jenneman said. "That should be the purpose of the college as a whole, too."

The Dennos dream dated back to 1971, when the Okerstrom Fine Arts Building was constructed. NMC leaders knew even then that Traverse City and the college needed a gallery and a cultural events space. The plan was to add each as wings to the Okerstrom Fine Arts Building someday in the future, when funds for such a project might become available. Other priorities always took precedence, though, even into the early 1980s, when an analysis by the Traverse Area Arts Council again identified formal exhibition space as woefully lacking in northwestern Michigan.

That changed in 1983 when the Fine Arts Building's namesake and NMC Trustee Shirley Okerstrom backed a plan to build a museum center separate from the arts department. The consensus was that such a community gem should be built where the entire community, not just students and faculty, could easily access it. With funding from Mike and Barb Dennos to hire architect Bob Holdeman; with the hiring of Jenneman; with the support of Rotary Charities, community leaders, former Governor Bill Milliken and his wife, Helen; and with state governmental support, the Dennos Museum Center opened in July of 1991.

Initially, the Milliken Auditorium was to have 250 seats, but a fundraiser advertised the space at 350 seats, and so the project was expanded to include this larger number—but at an increased cost of $1 million. There was some grumbling about the expense, but later those same naysayers agreed that not only was the increase wise but also the auditorium could have been made even larger and the community would still fill seats.

With its three changing exhibit galleries, elegant sculpture court, hands-on Discovery Gallery, renowned Inuit Gallery, and the Milliken Auditorium, the Dennos Museum Center was more than just a gallery and an event space; it became a premier cultural facility serving all of northern Michigan.

OsuitokIpeelie, Caribou, *c. 1995. Part of the noted Inuit art collection at the Dennos Museum Center.*

Among the museum center's permanent collections are Inuit prints and sculptures and Canadian Woodland Indian art. The Inuit collection comprises more than one thousand stone-cut, stencil, and lithograph prints, as well as sculptures, drawings, tools, and textiles from the late 1950s to the present. According to Director Jenneman, the collection reveals the vision and scope of contemporary Inuit art through both first-generation masters and new artists.

"This is the collection that put the museum on the map, nationally and even internationally," Jenneman said. "It's what makes us unique. In the region, we're so much more than our Inuit collection, but it is what puts the Dennos on a national stage."

The Canadian Woodland Indian Art collection contains pieces noted for conveying First Nation beliefs. Works from both of these noteworthy collections are frequently loaned to other museums as traveling exhibitions, allowing people all around the country to appreciate what NMC has identified as culturally significant.

The Dennos Museum Center today is not only a showcase for performance and visual arts but also the site of a variety of community events. More than six thousand K–12 students come through the museum every year. And, through the museum center, the college has hosted an incredible range of visitors, from astronauts and journalists to Appalachian Trail hikers and politicians, both foreign and domestic. Their time on campus, usually in a community lecture setting, followed by a question-and-answer session held inside Milliken Auditorium, has brought global views, experiences, and opinions to Traverse City otherwise unavailable to the community.

The college's Student Government Association and the International Affairs Forum lectures have brought many important voices to local audiences over the past twenty years, most hosted at the Dennos Museum Center. Among these notables were Terry Anderson, the Associated Press correspondent who was held hostage for seven years in Beirut; Floyd Cochran, a former member of the Aryan Nation who is now an antiracism activist; Patti Davis, daughter of former President Ronald Reagan, who wrote a book about growing up with Reagan as her father; and Arun Gandhi, grandson of Mohandas Gandhi, who cofounded the Mohandas K.

Gandhi Institute for Nonviolence. While its inviting and multiple-use buildings give the college an unparalleled facility in which to host these visitors, it is the Dennos Museum Center's addition to the main campus's academic atmosphere that has helped remake the college into a learning, as well as cultural, environment. The Dennos Museum Center has fulfilled its promise as a place where ideas can be shared, experienced, and discussed, where minds and hearts can learn about art, music, and history, bringing northern Michigan residents together with important creators from all around the world.

Sometime in the next twenty years, an expansion of the museum—in storage and gallery space—is sure to be considered, Jennman said.

"I personally would like to see the museum expanded," he said. "We're building our permanent collection now. We have an ongoing, changing program, and we need to have space to show it. Plus, we need space to dedicate to teaching collections, to move the museum more into the academic structure of the college. That's the future."

Front view of the Great Lakes Campus, with the Maritime Academy and Water Studies Institute on the left; Hagerty Center and the Culinary Institute on the right, 2008.

The Great Lakes Campus

"A SHOWCASE PROPERTY from every perspective." That's how Fred Laughlin, director of NMC's Culinary Institute, describes the college's newest addition, the Great Lakes Campus, located on East Front Street, west of the main campus. Built on eight acres with five hundred feet of West Bay frontage, the campus houses the Great Lakes Water Studies Institute, the Great Lakes Maritime Academy, the Great Lakes Culinary Institute, and the Hagerty Center.

"It's a focal point for Traverse City," says Board of Trustees Chairman Bob Brick. "It's one of NMC's accomplishments that I'm most proud of."

Brick, a realtor, and John Pelizzari, president of Fifth Third Bank of Grand Traverse, co-chaired the NMC Foundation's campaign to fund construction of the new campus. Brick says that it's difficult to imagine anyone actually missing the white cement freezer building that once hulked over this prime waterfront site, an eyesore that blocked the very view of Grand Traverse Bay that Traverse City is so famous for. To make way for the new campus, it was demolished in 2001.

Face the site today and what you see instead of a cement wall is a view restored. Undulating waves on West Bay seem to lap the shore, right through the glass-paneled center of the building. A brick exterior, a circular drive, and native grasses further ground the new facility in its surroundings—Sunset Park, the Traverse City Senior Center, and a harbor home to several teaching vessels. It's a setting that offers learning, recreational, and meditative opportunities for students, visitors, tourists, and even passers-by.

"It was purposefully designed as a public place that allows people to engage with the freshwater our region is known for," said President Nelson. "The board had a good vision when they planned the Great Lakes Campus."

Planners were cognizant of the need to conserve resources, too. Brick pointed out that the rubble of that cement freezer building wasn't discarded but rather crushed and used as foundational material for the new building.

The welcoming feeling of the Great Lakes Campus is more than just a nice view—it's important for our region, says one of its largest benefactors. "This region was built on nature and hospitality—all kinds of hospitality: culinary, hotel, entertainment, and simple neighborliness," said Wayne Lobdell, who along with his wife, Terry, helped fund the facility's teaching restaurant, Lobdell's. "This new home for the program fills a real ongoing need here."

Agricultural tourism grew in Michigan in the 1990s and during the first decade of the new millennium. That growth is expected to continue from 2012 and beyond. Traverse City has become known not just for its freshwater but also as a "foodie" destination; NMC's Great Lakes Culinary Institute is well-positioned to take advantage of this growing interest in fine, local, and creative food.

One way the college embraced this growing interest in fresh ingredients, imaginative recipes, and food preparation was by participating in Traverse City's Epicurian Classic, a community-wide event held annually at the Hagerty Center to promote the appreciation of fine food. From 2004 to 2008, NMC culinary students had the opportunity to rub elbows with renowned chefs visiting for the event. However, in 2008, the event attracted more than three thousand participants, making it too large for the Hagerty Center, and it was relocated. Still, during those

Great Lakes Culinary Institute student serving NMC employees (clockwise): Pauline Viall, Meg Young, Margaret Fox and Dean Jones at Lobdell's NMC's teaching restaurant, in 2005.

Maritime student lifeboat training, 2008.

five years, the students and faculty who participated in the Epicurian Classic gained valuable experience that continues to be put to use in special events now hosted at the Hagerty Center, from corporate dinners to formal receptions.

The Hagerty Center is also a state-of-the-art venue for professional conferences, meetings, seminars, and social gatherings, gives students real-world hospitality experience.

Along with the Great Lakes Culinary Institute and the Hagerty Center, the ninety-seven-thousand-square-foot campus is also the new home of the Great Lakes Maritime Academy. The academy offers coursework and degree programs in ship navigation and piloting, management of a ship's engine and mechanical operations, and shoreside careers. The academy was housed here in the old building and has a long and proud history as a degree program at NMC. Its new home builds on that history by offering many modernized and updated opportunities for students.

"The Great Lakes maritime industry is of tremendous importance to the region," said Trustee Doug Bishop, a former captain in the Naval Reserve. "The academy produces graduates essential to the industry, many of whom remain in the Grand Traverse area."

Paul LaPorte and George Bearup from Rotary Charities of Traverse City, presenting a $1 million check to NMC President Tim Nelson in support of the Water Studies Institute in 2004.

Rounding out the Great Lakes Campus is the NMC Water Studies Institute, which trains students to protect, conserve, and manage freshwater. Since 2008, it has been directed by Traverse City native Hans VanSumeren, a water researcher, nautical mission leader, and highly respected underwater vehicle pilot. Enrolled students can choose from three areas of study—economy and society, global policy, or science and technology—and all will use Grand Traverse County's forty-four inland lakes and 130-plus miles of shoreline as their classroom. The program gives students real-world training through hands-on coursework. Under VanSumeren's leadership, this training has led to discoveries lauded by freshwater scientists working in the field and prompted new directions in the study of water resources.

In the summer of 2009, water studies students conducted the first mapping of the bottom of Grand Traverse Bay in eighty years. They confirmed a 1980 shipwreck and created a depth map of East Bay using the new side-scan sonar equipment aboard the program's research vessel, *Northwestern*. In the summer of 2010, students continued the project in West Bay, providing immediately useful

The research vessel Northwestern *used by the Water Studies progam on Grand Traverse Bay, 2009.*

data to fisheries, commercial navigation mapmakers, and environmental impact assessment groups. The project located a second shipwreck, too, one previously unidentified. A team of operational divers from the NMC nautical archaeology program inspected the ship and identified the vessel as the *B West*, a barge that sank near Northport in 1957.

"The program combines people who are excited and passionate about this kind of work with the assets of northern Michigan and gives students immediate experiences they could never get even in two years at a big university," VanSumeren said.

Parsons-Stulen Technical Education Center (M-TEC)

IN 1959, when preparing for the North Central Association exam that would give the college its first national accreditation, the college was focused not on trade studies but on more traditional academics. In the 1980s and 1990s, students began asking for four-year degree programs, and NMC responded with the University Center in 1995. By the mid- to late 1990s, the need for traditional academics and for four-year degree programs certainly didn't go away, but the demand for mechanical and industrial trade skills grew, providing a solid impetus for a technical center.

Tourism and services still dominated the region's economy, but there was considerably more need for those skilled in general manufacturing and machine maintenance, and auto supply manufacturing opportunities were growing, too. Given the region's swift population growth, residential and commercial construction was also on the rise in the 1990s, providing employment for those skilled in heating, ventilation, and air conditioning.

Sculptor Robert Purvis surrounded by Dottie & Frank Stulen on his right and John & Betty Parsons, at the dedication of the Duet *sculpture, Parsons-Stulen Michigan Technical Education Center (M-TEC), 2001.*

While trades like these had not been on the minds of NMC's founders, forty years later, things had changed. Along with teachers, nurses, and paralegals, these were also the kinds of jobs that the region wanted, and so the Traverse City Area Chamber of Commerce supported NMC's application to the state for grant funds to open a technical education center. When state officials visited NMC in the late 1990s as part of the application process, they were shocked to be greeted by a standing-room-only crowd of supporters at Milliken Auditorium.

"It made a *great* impression," said Hal VanSumeren, president of the Traverse City Area Chamber of Commerce.

It must have, because NMC's application was one of eight selected to receive $4.4 million for a new technical education center. The state grant together with bond money funded construction costs for the technical education center, and the NMC Foundation raised money for equipment and an endowment.

Named in honor of John T. Parsons and Frank L. Stulen, two Traverse City inventors of numeric controls for the Parsons Corporation, the Parsons-Stulen Technical Education Center opened in January of 2001. Its sixty-five-thousand-square-feet included programs in information technology (network administration and database management), manufacturing (drafting and design, machine tool, electronics), construction (carpentry, HVACR, electrical), manufacturing technology, and

Program Coordinator Bill Queen with the Mobile Energy Demonstration Lab, 2006.

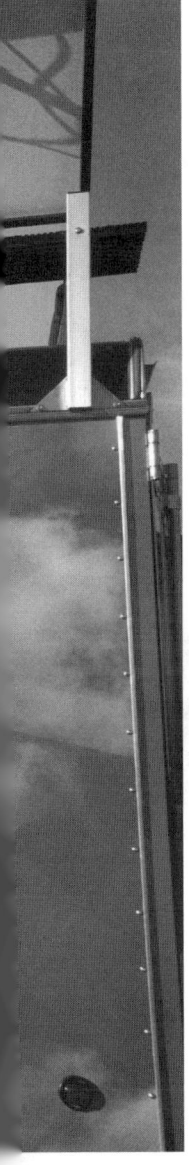

aviation (career pilot). Curriculum was based on input from many of the businesses that technical center graduates would eventually be working for.

Where better for NMC to experiment with using technology to teach than in a technical education center? Parsons-Stulen was NMC's opportunity to use the latest technology to teach students interested in electronics, mechanics, and computers. So course options included on-site training but also open learning (self-paced modules), interactive television (ITV), online classes, and a mobile computer lab, as well as the traditional classroom instruction.

VanSumeren credited the facility for bringing technology jobs to Traverse City, and the center's new director promised that the real-world, viable skills students gained would be immediately put to use in the workplace.

"The extent of our offerings is equal to our partnerships with business and industry," Executive Director Kirk Hornburg said. "We want instructors who are in the field."

The technical center made good on that promise in the first few years of its operation. Then, in the mid-2000s, some of the very manufacturers for which the Parsons-Stulen Center was designed to provide skilled workers were hit hard by the recession and downsized or went out of business completely. The technical center reassessed its function.

In 2004, as the price of traditional fuels began to rise, greater emphasis was put on renewable-energy training, and courses in solar, wind, biodiesel, and geothermal technologies were added. In 2005, NMC received a $450,000 grant from the Michigan Public Service Commission's Energy Efficiency Fund to establish an Energy Demonstration Center. It opened in September of

Invitation to the grand opening of the Parsons-Stulen Michigan Technical Education Center (M-TEC), February 8, 2001.

2005 and functioned as an educational umbrella for various advanced energy technology programs of study.

Today, Parsons-Stulen administrators, teachers, and students work with businesses and industry to provide the most current training in manufacturing, construction, aviation, and information technology. For example, when Electro-Optics, a Traverse City manufacturer of laser system components, needed training for its employees, the company turned to NMC's Technical Division, a part of Parsons-Stulen. And when the Grand Traverse region's Habitat for Humanity wanted to build its first-ever Leadership in Energy and Environmental Design (LEED) house, NMC students and faculty at Parsons-Stulen helped make it a reality.

"Innovation like this is exactly what has kept our country and our region moving forward," said NMC Trustee Elaine Wood. "This is what our college is all about."

Bill Queen discussing the use of solar energy with U.S. Senator Carl Levin, Marguerite Cotto, Ed Bailey, and Steve Morse, 2007.

Aero Park Laboratories Opens

THE NEWEST BUILDING on NMC's Aero Park Campus, the Aero Park Laboratories, opened for classes in January of 2011, housing NMC's renewable energy and construction technology programs.

Fittingly, the renovation of the building meets LEED certification standards. Highlights include a forty-five-foot wind tower and solar panels on the property, recycled construction waste, highly efficient insulation in the roof and walls, and renewable and locally sourced finish materials.

Hallway at the University Center showing some four-year college partners.

ACADEMIC ACHIEVEMENT

From Terms to Semesters

Northwestern Michigan College

Terms to semester conversion guide (Switch), 1994.

From Terms to Semesters

From its very beginning, NMC's school year was traditionally divided into four ten-week terms. In the fall of 1994, however, the college changed its academic calendar and divided the year into two sixteen-week semesters and one shortened summer session.

This change seemed logical enough; it aligned the college's schedule with that of twenty-eight other Michigan community colleges and most of the state's four-year institutions. One of NMC's main functions throughout its history—serving freshman and sophomore transfer students—became easier. By the early 1990s, most public four-year colleges and universities in the state were on semesters, and if NMC followed suit, it would make for an easier transfer of academic credits. The schedule change also pleased many local families with students enrolled at both NMC and local public or private secondary schools, since the new schedule now mirrored that of many area school districts.

But scheduling aside, changing from terms to semesters was a far more meaningful shift than just an alteration of the educational calendar. It necessitated nothing short of a complete curriculum overhaul. A Conversion Committee was established with eight faculty, two administrators, a counselor, a member of the library staff, a student, and a support staff member. A survey in November of 1990 found that both students and faculty favored the switch.

"This move will enable NMC to strategically place itself in a stronger position to build partnerships with four-year universities and K–12 districts," a report to President Tim Quinn from committee members Lynn Wonnacott, Diane Emling, and Roberta Teahen stated. "It is our belief that we must now get on with the work of a conversion, and that this be given the time, focus and priority it deserves."

Although they supported it in theory, faculty and staff needed to be consulted and encouraged to support the change in their classrooms if it was going to go smoothly. And initially, faculty and staff did have concerns. Could students, used to ten-week courses, maintain their focus over a full sixteen-week semester? Faculty Council Representative Stephen Drake expressed faculty concerns in a memo to President Quinn. Foremost was the fear that the college would attempt to make the move too quickly and students would suffer. A math professor, Drake said that in order to be successful, the transition would have to be treated more delicately than just a dry plus or minus math equation.

"A simple-minded approach that uses a 2/3 multiplier and a round-off will not work in every situation," Drake said, on behalf of the Faculty Council. "Wisdom and fairness must prevail."

It did. Along with the Conversion Committee, the college established the Core Curriculum Task Force in 1991 to study and define the requirements for an associate's degree across all disciplines. By 1993, the task force had identified general education requirements that focused on student outcomes rather than just time spent in the classroom. When these outcomes were considered, that time had to be quality time and well spent. Still, before the term-to-semester shift could be completed, sequential courses had to be revised so instructors would have fifteen weeks to work with students instead of just ten.

"It was probably the most significant look at the curriculum since NMC opened, because at the same time, we were also looking at the degree requirements," said Stephen Siciliano, vice president for educational services. "It gave us the opportunity to take a look at the entire curriculum in a fresh way. It was a very important step for us."

The process that started with an idea in 1990 was instituted in the fall of 1994, giving everyone enough time to prepare and adapt. Since then, unforeseen benefits and challenges for students and the community have surfaced. One of the challenges was Project Interconnect, an initiative begun in 1995 to link NMC and its University Center partners to fifteen area high schools via interactive television. Since the schedules between college and high school were more closely aligned, it was thought that this program would be popular, that high school students would be much more likely to participate, and that the program would increase membership. And then came the Internet, making television learning obsolete.

This did not catch NMC leaders unawares, however. During the same time period that Project Interconnect was being developed, the college was also building a flexible learning curriculum as part of the Michigan Virtual Learning Collaborative. This program mixed telecourses with ITV courses and online classes. This turned out to be an astute decision, because Project Interconnect came just before the explosion of the personal computer and the growth of the Internet and was not as successful as expected. Instead, it was expensive and relatively short-lived, while the flexible learning curriculum gained momentum and is still an active part of NMC today, involving dual-enrolled high school students and others. It has become a vibrant and useful portion of all of NMC's academic offerings.

With concurrent schedules, high school students also are much more likely to dual enroll in college courses while they are still in high school, adding to NMC's diverse student body. In January 2011, Governor Rick Snyder announced plans for education reform in Michigan, listing the opportunity for high school students to begin earning an associate's degree as a top priority. NMC has long made this option available to high schoolers, but with the calendar change it is now much easier for students to take advantage of it.

University Center Opening Doors faculty-staff celebration, 1995.

The University Center

THE 1995 OPENING of the University Center was a direct result of NMC's extensive community outreach efforts in the 1990s. A community-wide goal-setting process was undertaken in 1991 that looked at quality-of-life issues in the region. Called Grand Traverse 20/20, the initiative invited residents, leaders, businesses, and others to identify priorities for the future. One of the issues that scored highest was the opportunity to earn a four-year degree without leaving the Traverse City area. While that message sparked the drive to organize, fund, staff, and build the University Center, it turned out that the need stretched well beyond the five-county region.

Brochure explaining the University Center concept during the "Opening New Doors" campaign, 1994-95.

"I took a particular interest in this topic," said Elaine Wood, who served eighteen years on the board of trustees and was a recipient of the college's highest honor, the NMC Fellow. "There were so many benefits to having a community college—access and low cost, for example—and we didn't want to lose those. We wanted both. We wanted to have a community college and have advanced degrees. The idea was quite innovative at the time, but it wasn't difficult to get the college to agree to it. It was a win-win all around. It was an idea whose time had come."

The University Center's founding mirrored that of the college itself: an education institution with a history of responding to the needs of the community it served. A formal community assessment had shown that the lack of higher-education opportunities was a serious detriment to the region's growth and quality of life. This was not just an empty complaint but also an official finding of the 1988 Batelle study commissioned by the Traverse City Area Chamber of Commerce on how to attract better-paying jobs to the region. In the twenty-first-century economy, a four-year degree was standard in many professional workplaces. In addition, having a place to retrain employees locally, as workplace needs and wants shifted and technology advanced, became essential if Traverse City and the surrounding area were going to enjoy continued growth and a healthy economic development.

To employers seeking to locate a new business or to expand into a new area, only health care is more important than postsecondary education opportunities, according to the chamber's President Hal VanSumeren. The lack of those opportunities was a "glaring omission" in Traverse City prior to the opening of the University Center. But the benefits of such a facility would be there for students, too. Besides attracting employers, a better-educated workforce could demand more from the employers who needed their updated skills. These workers would be able to buy homes, pay taxes, dine out, and help the region thrive.

"When will you be four-year?" was the question that most consistently turned up in NMC's public opinion surveys and that President Quinn (1989–1994) said he heard most often in his conversations with community members in the early 1990s. After the Batelle study of 1988 and Grand Traverse 20/20 of 1991 both identified four-year degrees as something important missing from the area, Quinn organized his own focus group. Not to study the situation this time, but to act.

Quinn helped convene Founders 21, a group drawn from the five-county region and named with a nod to both NMC's past and its future. Members of Founders 21 started talking about NMC with anyone willing to listen. They talked with their neighbors about educational needs, spoke in public forums held around the region, made themselves available to the media, fielded questions, and gathered responses wherever they went.

The unanimous conclusion of Founders 21 was to open a university center. In 1993, President Quinn asked the board of trustees to make this goal a priority, and the trustees enthusiastically agreed.

"I called the other colleges and shared with them what we were doing and invited them to participate," Quinn said. In case they viewed NMC as a competitor for students instead of a partner in education, he said, "I reminded them that our mission was to be a community college."

An introductory meeting was held in Traverse City in the dome of the Park Place Hotel, and each of the ten institutions Quinn had spoken with sent representatives to attend. The public was invited, too, and people showed up in droves.

"The people from the universities were just overwhelmed," Quinn said. "They couldn't believe the number of people who came to those meetings, and they took one look around and right off the bat, ten of those schools said, 'We want to be involved.'"

Frankfort resident Gail Nugent chaired the Benzie County Founders 21 committee. An elementary school teacher, she understood the need for higher education. After a year at Michigan State, she and her husband had returned to Benzie

County to run a family business. Nugent attended NMC for a year, but in order to complete her bachelor's degree in elementary education, she had to commute to East Lansing between 1968 and 1970, leaving her home Monday morning and returning Friday afternoon. A mother of two young children, Nugent was enthusiastic about joining in an effort that would allow future generations to pursue higher education without disrupting their families or jobs.

"I was certainly aware of the fact we needed something here beyond the two-year program," she said. "I was excited from the very beginning."

This observation echoed that of one of NMC's founders. Though Les Biederman died in 1986, he had anticipated this moment in the college's journey, writing about it in his 1982 autobiography, *Happy Days*.

"I have an idea for the college," he wrote. "I'm not trying to tell anybody what to do, just pointing out what might happen if anyone is in the mood for a little visionary future-building ... NMC could become an association of colleges, a university of satellite institutions of learning."

In August 1995, the University Center put that idea into practice and opened with 667 students enrolled. These first students were able to select courses from among forty-four programs from twelve partner colleges and universities. Those university partners have remained relatively stable over the years, and at the start of the spring 2012 term, the University Center had nine partners, with more than 50 degree opportunities.

The ability to study toward a four-year degree without leaving northern Michigan turned out to be an opportunity ripe for those beyond Grand Traverse County and even the surrounding counties' borders.

"The University Center experiment has been rather extraordinary," said Marguerite Cotto, vice president for lifelong and professional learning. "We've developed lots of creative ways to fill the postsecondary education need here in Traverse City and all the way to Escanaba in the Upper Peninsula, too."

Today, 25 percent of the University Center's students come from places outside the expected NMC service area of Grand Traverse, Leelanau, Benzie, Antrim, and Kalkaska counties. Students come from as far as Sault Ste. Marie and Escanaba.

The University Center opening in 1995 was one answer to the question of whether NMC would ever become a four-year institution. The question still persists today. It's a valid one, Cotto says.

"There is a lot of stability here with our member universities, and we are the region's resource for learning. In some signature disciplines, we should also be the resource for learning at the baccalaureate level."

Art Schmuckal with Ilse Burke and Tim Quinn at dedication ceremony naming the Schmuckal Building at the University Center in 1997.

Even though NMC's 2011 request to the state to be able to offer four-year nursing and four-year maritime degrees was initially denied, the quest will not end with that shortsighted answer. In the spring of 2012, the Michigan legislature was again considering a bill that would allow community colleges to offer some four-year degrees.

"The most important matter on our plate presently is the legislation pending in Lansing to allow community colleges in Michigan to award limited baccalaureate degrees," said Trustee Doug Bishop. "Funding and the ability to deliver education needed by our students at affordable prices will be an ongoing issue, and a collateral issue to that will be the ability to attract and retain top-notch staff and faculty."

Certainly the question "When will you be four-year?" remains a viable one for NMC leadership, faculty, and students alike and one that will likely be answered sometime in the college's next twenty years.

Four-Year Degree Partnerships

SPARKED BY COMMUNITY NEED, regionwide financial support, and those early phone calls by President Tim Quinn to reach out to colleges and universities across the state, today NMC has four-year degree partnerships with nine universities. These are Central Michigan University, Davenport University, Eastern Michigan University, Ferris State University, Grand Valley State University, Lawrence Technological University, Michigan State University, Spring Arbor University, and Western Michigan University.

Students studying varied disciplines from accounting, computer information technology, and hotel management to education, nursing, and social work can receive their bachelor's degree right here in Traverse City via these academic partnerships with four-year institutions. In addition, these same partnerships offer master's program opportunities to NMC students in administration, business, education, humanities, occupational therapy, organizational management, reading and literacy, school principalship, and social work. A doctoral degree is available in education through a partnership with Central Michigan University, and a wide variety of undergraduate and graduate certificates in programs from plant science to homeland security round out the offerings available to NMC students thanks to these educational partnerships.

"These partnerships benefit everyone: the community, the college, and our partner universities," said President Quinn, "Even if NMC does become a four-year college, the University Center would still thrive."

NMC students taking part in a two-week aviation course at the University of the West of England, 2011.

International Aviation

AVIATION WAS FIRST ADDED as a course of study back in 1967, becoming only the third college in the state to take to the air, so to speak. By 1991 there were two hundred students enrolled in the flight program, even though it was one of the more expensive educational options the college provided. Today, with NMC's growing focus on preparing students for a global world, the aviation program has been completely overhauled to become international in scope but without losing its tight-knit atmosphere.

Director of Aviation Aaron Cook says these two aspects of NMC's aviation program not only can, but must exist simultaneously.

"The program has always been relatively small, and to a certain extent that's been intentional. We attract people who want a personalized family atmosphere. Everybody gets to know everybody quite well, and that creates a useful skill set, as well as a lifelong relationship with the college. And although aviation is a global industry, it's also one where many people know each other and it really is quite small."

Cook himself is a product of that tight-knit community. He enrolled in the flight program in 1997, graduated in 2000, worked as both a flight instructor and an air services pilot, and then came back to NMC to direct the very program that trained him. He knows from personal experience that the family atmosphere at NMC prepares pilots for personal as well as professional success, both here and abroad.

"Crew resource management, the ability to work with the other people in the airplane, is crucial," Cook said. "If you're on a twelve-hour trip to China, you need to get along with people well because of the small environment. We've always fostered those skills; that's been part of the attractiveness of the program and one reason for the high quality of pilots the program has turned out."

In 2010, the aviation program began an international partnership with the United Kingdom to train UK students to be pilots here in the United States and to allow NMC aviation students to study abroad. Today, the international aviation program has partnerships with the University of Hertfordshire, London Metropolitan University, and the University of the West of England, all in the United Kingdom. An NMC delegation has planned a trip to India to investigate starting an aviation program partnership with their Aeronautical Engineering Institute, beginning as soon as the summer of 2012. The college has also fielded inquiries from a flight program in Beijing, China, and the aviation department at the University of Witwatersand in South Africa.

Other opportunities for students enrolled in aviation include charter, airline, and military pilot certification; flight instruction; and study and experience in the swiftly-growing field of unmanned aircraft.

"This is a very exciting area of study, and NMC is the only community college in the country training drone pilots," said Cook.

Unmanned aircrafts, or drones, have applications for the U.S. military and NASA but also for commercial business uses, such as checking on remote power lines, bridges, energy pipelines, and even windmills and cropland.

NMC Aviation fleet, 2003.

At right, NMC students, summer interns, and local residents with WSI instructor Dr. Constanza Hazelwood, fourth from left, in Costa Rica, 2011.

NMC's aviation program now also offers training toward FAA ratings and licenses including Private, Instrument, Commercial, Multiengine, and Flight Instructor. Partnerships with Davenport and Ferris State universities provide students additional opportunities in aviation coursework.

By 2014, the program could have as many as two hundred twenty-five students, Cook said, most of whom he predicted will be attracted to the college because of these new and cutting-edge opportunities.

New Degrees and Credentials

WITH THE OPENING of the Great Lakes Campus in 2003 and 2004, degree opportunities for NMC students expanded immediately because there was new space for study. But it was passion, history, a sense of stewardship, and geography, that prompted NMC to add another degree program to the facility in 2009: the Associate in Science and Arts degree for Freshwater Studies. That's a long description for an ambitious and first-of-its-kind initiative on global water management designed to prepare students to enter the workforce or transfer to a four-year school.

"No other community college in the country has this unique set of institutional and human resources and certainly not this privileged location for a learning laboratory," said Hans VanSumeren, the Water Studies Institute's director.

Impending water shortages around the world could make our local resource even more valuable in the coming decades, and with the new freshwater studies degree program, NMC saw an opportunity to take a lead in teaching students how to manage local, national, and even worldwide water resources.

"We want to support our students so they can compete favorably in a global economic environment," said Dr. Constanza Hazelwood, education and outreach coordinator for the Water Studies Institute. "In a region where water is abundant, we can readily forget that it is a scarce resource in so many areas of the globe."

Students choose one of three concentrations within the program: science and technology, global freshwater policy and sustainability, or economy and society. The freshwater studies degree will allow students to build on existing NMC courses such as watershed science and oceanography. After speaking with potential employers in the summer of 2009, VanSumeren suggested that NMC add marine technician and coastal brownfield technician to the program, which it did.

New courses, Introduction to Water Studies and Introduction to GIS (Geographic Information Systems), were added, giving students enrolled in the program the opportunity to participate in extensive field experiences and to apply for internships. For example, in the summer of 2011, NMC partnered with EARTH University and sent five Water Studies Institute students to Costa Rica to study the role of communities in good water management.

Opportunities for degree programs have continued to grow and change over the past two decades for virtually all NMC students—and not just those studying water management and the culinary arts. Since 2000, there has been an increased emphasis on adding nationally-recognized certification requirements and opportunities to degree programs.

"Particularly in the past ten years there has been a new focus on external validation," said Stephen Siciliano, vice president for educational services. "This certainly helps with transferring, placement and will continue to be part of what an NMC education provides."

In 2001, as part of a workforce collaboration with Munson Healthcare, NMC offered a pharmacy technician independent study program. This was a natural addition to NMC's growing healthcare curriculum, said health occupations instructor and administrator Jean Rokos.

"Our health occupations faculty are really involved on the local, state, and national level, so we know what's needed, and we're able to bring best practices here to NMC," she said. "Whether it's the dental program, our allied health and our nursing programs, or this new independent study, we have a wide variety of students who are able to be successful here, and that's a really good feeling."

In the fall of 2004, the Great Lakes Maritime Academy added a power systems program to train graduates to operate power plants. In 2008, an insurance studies program was added, with certificates available in personal insurance, life and health insurance, and commercial insurance. In the spring of 2010, construction technology added certificates in carpentry, electrical, HVAC/R, and facilities management.

From 2000 to the present, advancements were also made in NMC's automotive services program in order to keep up with real-world needs. Walk into an automotive garage today and some of the tools and equipment that are standard issue might not even have existed a decade ago. As the U.S. government has demanded higher fuel efficiency and lower emissions on cars and trucks and as drivers have demanded more comfort and better technology, our vehicles have become complex machines increasingly powered by new fuels and more efficient engines and controlled by built-in computers. These new vehicles might live up to their manufacturer's promise of being longer lasting, but they will still need regular maintenance and repair. Enter the modern-day auto tech student, who, because of this advancing automotive technology, now often needs three full years of coursework to earn an associate's degree.

In 2007, the college added an Electrical and Drivability Specialist Certificate to its already available Master Automotive Technician Certificate so that students could realize certain accomplishments after as little as a year of training in the program. In 2011, NMC added a Hybrid Automotive Technology Certificate, which gave students an opportunity to train for one of the fastest-growing segments of the market. Because of these changes and program additions, NMC's automotive students can be assured of receiving instruction and training relevant to the real needs of today's high-tech jobs.

In the computer information technology (CIT) program, NMC added a CIT developer associate's degree and a CIT infrastructure associate's degree in 2007 to the department's existing CIT general degree. A CIT general is aimed at students who want to transfer to another institution in order to pursue a four-year degree. For students with specific interests and career goals in programming, database, desktop, web development,

NMC Automotive instructor David Bajema working with Hybrid Technology students in 2011.

certification-based hardware, and network administration, an associate's degree in these focused areas offers more immediately marketable skills. Also in 2007, NMC offered three progressive Infrastructure Specialist Certificates for nondegree students.

In 2010 NMC broke academic ground again by offering the area's first viticulture certification program. Viticulture is the science, production, and study of grapes, and just as geography made both the freshwater studies and the Maritime Academy a natural fit for the college, so, too, for viticulture. Michigan's climate offers a unique challenge for winemakers; it's one of the few places in the world where commercial wineries thrive even in cool weather. Until the NMC program, the area's grape and wine industry had no source for workers trained in the harsh winter conditions we experience here along the forty-fifth parallel. Thanks to a new partnership among NMC, Michigan State University, and the online VESTA (Viticulture and Enology Science and Technology Alliance) program at Missouri State University, that training is now being provided. Students can earn a viticulture certificate at the University Center from Michigan State University, with an option to complete an associate's degree from NMC. All classes are offered online or in Traverse City at the University Center.

Students who enroll take general education credits at NMC, pursue their VESTA classes online, and arrange internships through MSU at one or more of the two dozen wineries in northwest Michigan. As a boost to the program, the National Science Foundation awarded funding to VESTA to pay for students to attend state and national viticulture conferences.

A winning combination of student interest, specific industry demand, present and future career opportunities, and NMC's ability to deliver learning opportunities has led to all of the new degree and certificate curriculum additions the college has added since 1991.

Extended Education

JOIN A FLUTE CHOIR, master Microsoft Excel, brush up on your conversational Spanish, learn to make an authentic sushi roll, or chart your family's genealogy. Braid a rug, study portrait photography, learn database management, design a web page, or learn to prepare the peasant foods of Tuscany. All these opportunities and more are available to the Extended Education Services (EES) student at NMC.

Ready-to-use skills taught by instructors with real-world experience offering students new competency in as little as three hours distinguish the hundreds of annual EES courses. It is perhaps this department of NMC that best exemplifies the college's commitment to lifelong learning and community outreach.

Noncredit courses were part of the original mission articulated by the college founders back in 1951. By 1976, EES's course catalog proclaimed, "Education: Not a Task to Be Completed but a Process to Be Continued." By 2001, that headline was simplified yet still conveyed the core message: "Learn for Life." Today, EES is committed to "Lifelong Learning."

The essence of EES throughout its history echoes President Nelson's admonitions to "keep learning at the center of everything we do at NMC." Some learners at NMC aren't looking for a degree but rather to master their home computer, add social networking to their marketing strategies at work, or paint a lakeside landscape.

"It's a face of the college," Director Carol Evans said. "In the last ten years, even in the last five years, there's been a greater attempt to truly use this resource," she said. "There is a deeper awareness by the community of the college as a whole."

While extended education is only one way the college reaches out to the community, to the many EES students who have never set foot in a dorm or the library or even visited the Dennos Museum, it is their one entry point to NMC. In 2001, EES enrollment reached nearly eighty-seven hundred diverse students. These students took 933 different courses, almost ten times the ninety-eight courses offered in NMC's first EES catalog published back in 1976. In 2011, that enrollment was higher still, with almost nine thousand students taking a vast array of different but enriching courses.

EES contains programs aimed at a wide audience and divided into different segments: the Senior Academy, offering courses designed for students aged fifty-five and over; the College for Kids, a summer enrichment, entertainment, and skill-building program for students as young as four and five; and professional development courses, most focused on computer skills, to provide beneficial training that students otherwise might have to travel to obtain.

Evans said she and EES staff brainstorm ideas for classes, but she also fields calls from NMC instructors who have creative ideas and are seeking to share their knowledge and skills with EES students, whether they are sculpting, cooking, traveling abroad, or introducing a new technology.

Because courses change frequently, EES can be more agile in scheduling, able to respond quickly to demand. Evans said that tendency to change frequently is a stated goal. Each term the division strives to make 15 percent of its offerings new. This keeps EES fresh and keeps many students reenrolling in new classes, truly embracing that "Learn for Life" motto.

NMC's Aviation program underwent a complete transformation during recent years.
The program is now a model for others to follow, and is gaining international renown.

The annual Taster's Guild at NMC is a highly-anticipated event that earns tens of thousands dollars for the college's Great Lakes Culinary Institute.

NMC's Great Lakes Campus is home to the college's Maritime, Culinary and Water Studies programs, the Hagerty Center, and Lobdell's: A Teaching Restaurant and a welcome addition to the Traverse City shoreline.

Lobdell's: A Teaching Restaurant is not only a great showcase and learning opportunity for culinary students but an incredible setting for area diners.

View of the State of Michigan, *the research vessel* Northwestern *and NMC's seaplane at the college's Great Lakes Campus on West Grand Traverse Bay.*

The research vessel Northwestern *docked at NMC's Great Lakes Campus.*

STUDENT LIFE

The Pulse of a Growing College

Northwestern Michigan College

Clubs & Special Interests

"NOTHING EVER BECOMES REAL," the poet John Keats said, "until it is experienced." All students at NMC have the opportunity to augment their formal study with the social and real-life experiences offered by a wide variety of student groups, clubs, and societies.

From the Engineering Club and the Jane Addams Social Work Advocacy Group to the Web Slingers and Women on the Water, more than forty diverse groups invite NMC student involvement. Mr. Keats himself may have appreciated the Live Poets Society, a weekly round table and creative lab where participants write, recite, and experiment with poetry, or Radio Theater, a group offering students experience in writing, editing, and performing dramas live on the campus FM station, WNMC.

Students who don't see a group they're interested in joining are encouraged by the college to start a new one and to invite

like-minded others to join them. All that's needed to be officially recognized is a faculty advisor, a contact person, a description of the group, and a promise that the new group will be open to all NMC students.

NMC recently formalized the process of starting an official student group both to insure good communication between the new group and the administration and to offer the group valuable campus services. Official NMC groups have access to facilities for their activities and meetings, are eligible to sponsor campus events, have the opportunity to use college advertising and promotional resources, are assigned a campus address, are listed on NMC's website, and are eligible for funding. Both the Student Government Association and the Student Incubation Fund make money available for some club activities. Both new and existing groups are encouraged to seek out this funding, via a simple application process.

The Student Government Association is a group of currently enrolled students who represent NMC's entire student body. Each academic discipline selects a representative, and the entire student body also elects three at-large students. This group meets weekly to discuss student issues.

Participation in student groups offers a bit of the experience Keats referenced and at NMC can include everything from socializing and career insight to political experience and adventure. For example, members of NMC's Engineering Club not only participated in the Blizzard Baja race held in the Upper Peninsula in Houghton, Michigan, in 2006, but also won first place. Sponsored by Michigan Technological

University, the Blizzard Baja race consists of two hour-and-a-half dune buggy winter endurance races over a rigorous track made of snow and ice. Competing in subzero temperatures, Engineering Club members bested competitors from twenty-two other schools.

East Hall Fire

Developments on the college's campus from 1991 to 2011 were almost all accomplishments to celebrate, with one major exception. On Easter weekend in April of 1998, a dormitory fire caused life-threatening injuries to one NMC student, required eight other students to be treated for smoke inhalation, and displaced dozens more. The fire damaged the lobby of East Hall between North Tower and South Tower and also caused extensive damage to South Tower, which remained closed for almost a year.

A former student, who admitted to abusing alcohol, was arrested after he confessed to starting the fire on a dare. He eventually pled guilty to arson and was sentenced to ten years in prison.

Prior to the fire, serious crime was virtually unheard of on NMC's campus. In the weeks and months following the fire, college leaders responded by revisiting certain policies and increasing dorm security. Prior to the fire, the dorms had been equipped with fire alarms, but because false alarms were relatively common, many students didn't take the alarms seriously. As a remedy, the college installed video cameras in the hallways and promised to prosecute anyone who pulled a fire alarm as a prank. A new policy called for automatic expulsion of any student caught doing so.

Funds from an insurance settlement were used to repair the structural damage to East Hall, install a sprinkler system, and add new fire alarms as well as new strobe light alarms for the hearing impaired. The dorm's lobby was rebuilt, and a new student center was added to East Hall's neighbor, West Hall.

A speaker from Collegiate Consultants on Drugs and Alcohol was invited to visit the campus and speak to students on the dangers of alcohol, new alcohol abuse training was required of dorm staff, and fire drills were mandatory once a month, with required dorm resident participation.

Because the student who caused the fire admitted to being intoxicated at the time of the crime, NMC also reassessed its policy regarding student drinking. Alcohol was already banned on campus before the fire, but in the months afterward, NMC became the first college in the state to adopt a policy of calling police to investigate underage drinking rather than handling it in-house.

If there is a happy ending to this episode, it was that the student who was burned not only recovered but also returned to classes and went on to graduate from NMC.

Parking Progress

If there's one single problem that has dogged NMC's main campus throughout its history; if there's one problem faced by students, faculty, and visitors alike; and if there's one problem that is indicative of NMC's overall success in other areas, it would be this: the problem of finding a parking space.

Although the parking problem is most evident on the main campus, this issue has sometimes popped up on other campuses as well. For example, when the Great Lakes Campus opened in 2003, some people attending functions next door at the Traverse City Senior Center complained that they couldn't find a parking space anymore if there was an event going on at the campus's Hagerty Center. Asking senior citizens to park across busy Front

Parking Patrol, outside of Osterlin Library in the late 1990s.

Street's four lanes and walk back to the senior center wasn't a good option. A partial solution was to pave an additional lot near the Great Lakes Campus and to urge patrons not to park at the senior center, but some nights, parking there is still at a premium.

Sharp spikes in student numbers have translated into more traffic on campus. Often, either students don't like to carpool or it isn't practical because of their varied schedules. When the spring semester of 2010 began in January of that year, NMC broke enrollment records again, and the parking problem intensified.

NMC Security Director Michael Hoffman hired temporary workers to staff the main campus parking lots for the first two weeks of classes. In 2011, a temporary parking lot was set up in the campus baseball field, and after some back-and-forth negotiating, NMC administrators worked with Bay Area Transportation Authority administrators to set up fixed routes to the college, with the idea of encouraging more students to use public transportation.

Over the past twenty years, parking has been addressed in various ways, none of which has completely solved the problem of finding a parking space.

Rack card for the tobacco-free campus initiative in 2010.

A Tobacco-Free Campus

On May 1, 2010, Michigan became one of twenty-four states to ban smoking in public places. The Dr. Ron Davis Law, part of the Michigan Clean Indoor Air Act, made it a misdemeanor to smoke in any public place in the state, including workplaces, restaurants, malls, and bars. Violators who ignored warnings were subject to $100 and $500 fines. The new law also banned smoking in public meetings, at government agencies, on the patios of restaurants, and in all schools.

When this law went into effect, NMC already had a smoking policy in place, adopted in December of 1996 and revised in 2001, 2006, and 2007, that banned smoking in classrooms and in campus buildings but didn't address other uses of tobacco. In the interest of providing a safe, healthy, and clean environment for students, employees, and visitors and in accordance with the new state law, NMC went completely smoke free August 30, 2010. Now, the use or the sale of any tobacco products, including chewing tobacco, is prohibited both indoors and outside on all NMC properties. Students, faculty, and staff who were smokers had a choice of either quitting smoking altogether or smoking only before entering campus or after leaving.

The college did address the physical and emotional needs of those working to quit their tobacco habit. The tobacco-free policy included a plan for helping students and faculty over their initial withdrawal difficulties. NMC supported those who wanted to quit by offering a variety of resources, including free workshops, support groups, and counseling sessions. The college even provided some cessation aids, such as nicotine gum, for free. Also, some employees on NMC's health plan were eligible for reimbursed treatment and cessation aids as well. Today, all of NMC's campuses are totally tobacco free. However, enforcement of the policy remains very much a work in progress.

List of 21,000 donors to NMC since its founding, displayed at 60th anniversary "Thank You" celebration, Hagerty Center, 2011.

MONEY MATTERS

Sustaining and Thriving

Northwestern
Michigan
College

60th Anniversary commemorative pin for donors and friends of NMC, 2011.

A "Culture of Philanthropy"

Ask NMC's BOARD OF TRUSTEES Chairman Bob Brick which of NMC's many accomplishments he's proudest of and he'll say balancing an annual budget that has grown to more than $42 million. Brick said he's especially proud that the college has been able to balance its budget while also responding well to a rapidly growing student body with increasingly complex educational needs.

"It's no longer just a chalkboard and an eraser," Brick said. "It's computers and all forms of technology."

Fiscal prudence even in the face of rapidly growing learning needs wouldn't be possible without what another of NMC's leaders, Kathleen Guy, calls a "culture of philanthropy." Both Brick and Guy say that NMC's financial support has come from a variety of sources, including community donors, businesses, and granting institutions but also from students, faculty, and staff.

"Everybody's bought into what we are trying to do," said Brick, "which is lift life up here for everyone through education. Access to learning is really the thread that runs through all disciplines. And that costs money."

Guy, who retired from NMC in June 2011, worked as executive director of the NMC Foundation and as vice president for institutional advancement, among other positions. One of her biggest accomplishments was developing the college's annual campaign.

"People love to give to people," Guy said, "and people here feel a sense of ownership about NMC that is fairly unique among community colleges. It goes back to our earliest days when the people of Traverse City said, 'We want a college here, and we'll do whatever it takes to make that happen.' That is also our challenge for the future. To continue to live up to that vision."

That's because, Guy says, many of the people who helped fund NMC in its beginning years are gone now. So new people, new donors, will need to carry out their vision. Will those new people be the children and grandchildren of the original founders? Will they be a new generation of people who have moved to northern Michigan? Or will they be NMC's alumni? "Yes, yes, and yes," says Guy. "They will be all those things."

Founded as a nonprofit corporation in 1981, the NMC Foundation accepts contributions on behalf of the college in four main areas: excellence, scholarships, capital projects, and faculty/staff enrichment. Governed by a board of directors composed of an executive committee, general members, honorary members, emeritus members, faculty representatives, and a student representative, the foundation is an umbrella for all sorts of personal gifts to the college. From the Annual Campaign for Scholarships and Programs, memorial gifts, matching gifts, and planned giving to gifts for specific programs and facilities, scholarships, and sponsorships, the foundation manages these gifts so they can be used to benefit the entire NMC community.

In 2008, the foundation celebrated reaching a big milestone: awarding $1 million in total scholarship dollars to students in all sixty NMC programs of study.

This was also the year that the first scholarships from the Margaret Furney estate were awarded. Furney was a retired teacher who believed strongly enough in the value of higher education to leave NMC $1.1 million in her will to fund scholarships for single parents. With her gift, she joined a diverse group of donors with one thing in common: a desire to help people further their education. At NMC, scholarship giving draws donors from all walks of life, from the famous (for example, in 1976 singer Gordon Lightfoot established scholarships for Great Lakes Maritime cadets) to the not-so famous. Whatever the origin of the gift, scholarships mean the same thing to all of the grateful recipients: the opportunity to learn.

Lena Jensen's Gift

IN THE PAST TWENTY YEARS, financial support for NMC has come from all the logical sources: state aid, local taxes, grant-making foundations, wealthy community leaders, small donors, art-lovers, and successful businesses, to name a few. But in 1996, one large gift came from a surprising source.

When Traverse City resident Lena Jensen died at the age of eighty-nine, she had never married and had no children or close family members. A private woman who kept mostly to herself, Jensen had moved to Traverse City in 1934 with just a suitcase and $5. But she did have dreams.

Lena Jensen wanted to live in a log cabin, and she wanted young people to be able to go to college even if, like herself, they didn't come from a wealthy background. Jensen never did get the opportunity to go to college, but she did own a log cabin. With the money she earned working as first a nanny and then a housekeeper and at various jobs for Munson Hospital, J&S Hamburg, and Parts Manufacturing, Jensen bought herself a tiny log cabin on Clinch Street in Traverse City.

When she died in 1998, she willed the house to her church and $175,000 to NMC. The college established the Lena C.

Jensen Scholarship in her honor, which now makes annual awards of $1,000 to selected full- and part-time students.

The foundation also administers Innovation Grants, a fund for faculty, staff, and students with innovative initiatives that require start-up funding. "Great things have come from these grants," said NMC Board of Trustees Vice Chair William Myers, who serves on the grant-making committee. "Rewarding innovative thinking is such a positive part of what NMC does."

By 2009, $50,000 had been awarded to a dozen different projects, including purchasing a submersible laser scanner, inviting an artist-in-residence to the Dennos Museum Center, and expanding the capacity of the Writing and Reading Center. By 2010 the NMC Foundation board agreed to make up to $75,000 available annually to fund student, faculty, and staff proposals.

"Our students need to be prepared for a knowledge-based economy and a world where change is constant. The best way to do that is to cultivate innovation among them," said Guy of the work of the NMC Foundation.

Besides helping to fund NMC, the foundation also gives out its annual Foundation Excellence Award to recognize those who truly exemplify NMC values in their daily work. The foundation also organizes an annual scholarship luncheon, so that donors and recipients can meet each other, and the

Scholarship Open, the largest golfing fundraiser in the area. In 2011 more than two hundred golfers and dozens of sponsors raised more than $62,000 for NMC Honors, Presidential, and Divisional scholarships. Since it began in 1980, the tournament has raised more than $1 million.

In 2001, the NMC Foundation was recognized as among the top 20 percent of community college foundations nationwide for its fundraising efforts. It placed first in terms of endowment market value per student, twelfth for dollars raised per student, and thirty-second for total dollars raised. In 2011, the foundation celebrated its thirtieth anniversary. Guy said that she expects the group to get stronger in the coming years because of the leadership it enjoys.

"Our future success is going to rely on the leaders we surround ourselves with," she said. "There are forty committed, aligned people on the board now. They're active and engaged. There isn't a single person there who isn't a donor to the college. They're all believers. And that's one of the things about which I am most proud."

The NMC Foundation, she said, is poised and ready for the next set of challenges.

Annual Campaign for Scholarships and Programs

THE ANNUAL CAMPAIGN for Scholarships and Programs provides vital support for scholarships, programs, facilities, and special projects. The campaign offers a way for individual donors and businesses to seed the future educational ground of northern Michigan by pledging their financial support in both large and small gifts.

With government budgets increasingly tight, state funding shrinking, and enrollment growing, the annual campaign funds many scholarships that often make the difference for students who might not otherwise be able to attend college. The campaign also recruits and organizes those individuals and

One of the last commencements "under the pines" in front of the library, 1993.

businesses willing to match donations offered by first-time givers, doubling their impact.

Despite Michigan's economic doldrums and the ensuing impact on state funding for community colleges, NMC has continued to thrive partly because of its successful private and community fundraising efforts. For example, the college received $8.8 million in state aid in 2008—the same amount it received eight years prior, in 2000. Costs for a college education certainly rose in those eight years, and the number of students at NMC grew, with no corresponding rise in state funding, due to Michigan's dire economy. Yet NMC was able to expand its services and programs while keeping average class size small and tuition and fee increases to a modest 3.2 percent. This was possible, in large part, because of the success of the NMC Foundation's annual campaign.

Every year the annual campaign sets an ambitious fundraising goal, and two volunteer campaign cochairs lead the effort in reaching it.

The Capital Campaigns

THERE'S AN APT SAYING popular with teachers that goes something like this: "Education is priceless." While true in theory, in actuality NMC administrators know that a high-quality education is expensive to provide.

To fund the advances in learning and technology; to pay for the design, construction, renovation, and maintenance of campus buildings; and to attract capable faculty and launch new programs, capital is needed. Over the past two decades, NMC has been successful in securing significant support from the state of Michigan and from Grand Traverse County voters. To augment these sources of funding, private donations were required if the college wanted to continue to respond to the needs of learners. In NMC's third twenty years, several capital campaigns were launched.

In February of 1994, the University Center Capital Campaign had a goal of raising $5.9 million to fund the development of a new campus, purchase needed technology, develop an electronic library for students, and establish an operating endowment. With the theme of "Buy a Brick, Build a Future," area residents and businesses were invited to buy a brick for $100 and become a "founder" of the University Center. The appeal was remarkably successful. At the close of the campaign, more than $8 million was raised, and the University Center opened in the fall of 1995 to an excited and supportive community of students and future students. It offered the promise of "Opening New Doors" to higher education for the people of northern Michigan by providing, for the first time, a chance for area residents to work toward a professional degree without leaving home.

In the fall of 2000, the NMC Foundation's Capital Campaign earmarked some of its funding for the Parsons-Stulen Technical Center, also known as M-TEC. While construction costs were covered by a state grant and the 1999 bond issue money, equipment and endowment needs remained. Those were addressed by the NMC Foundation's capital campaign that set and met its goal of raising $3 million by January 2001.

In the fall of 2003, NMC again launched an ambitious capital campaign to complete funding of a project supported by the state of Michigan and by Grand Traverse County voters. The Great Lakes Campus Capital Campaign, co-chaired by John Pelizzari and Bob Brick, set a goal of raising $2.95 million. In his appeal, the honorary chair, astronaut Jerry Linenger, of Suttons Bay, called attention to the importance of the new campus and its role in protecting our freshwater resources.

"From my perch in space living aboard the Russian space station Mir, I experienced a 'whole new view' of the planet," Linenger said. "I can vouch for the fact that there is no other part of the globe more recognizable, more spectacular, than the Great Lakes region."

Again the campaign reached out to all levels of donors. In addition to major individual and corporate donors, community members were invited to support the effort through a "Buy a Fish" campaign. A "spokesfish" even made appearances at the National Cherry Festival, as well as Friday Night Live, and gave service club presentations to raise awareness of the effort. For a $100 gift, a stainless steel fish was engraved with the donor's name and displayed in "schools" fastened onto wall panels throughout the new building.

The Commitment Scholarships

In its first twenty years (1951–1971), NMC concentrated on attracting and serving primarily traditional students: high school graduates seeking a higher education in order to prepare them for professional careers.

In its second twenty years (1971–1991), the college began reaching out to nontraditional students in larger numbers. These students included professionals seeking a second career or career advancement, workers needing updated skills training, older students who had never gone to college before, and retirees seeking training not necessarily for employment but rather for personal enrichment or to follow a longtime dream.

In this, its third twenty years (1991–2011), NMC continued to serve its diverse student body but also extended a welcoming hand to a new and overlooked group of potential students: those who wouldn't be ready for college for several years and who might not be able to afford it when the time came.

In 1993, the college began an innovative scholarship program aimed at academically promising middle school students with financial need. Unlike other scholarships, the Commitment Scholarships would not be awarded only to students with financial need and good academic performance but would also take into account other considerations. Students from single-parent homes, students who had a sibling or parent with a disability or chronic illness, and students who exhibited academic promise but weren't always able to realize that promise because of mitigating social factors would be among those considered.

The Commitment Scholarship initiative offered a full-tuition scholarship to seventh graders to attend NMC for

NMC Commitment Scholars on Chicago fieldtrip, 2007.

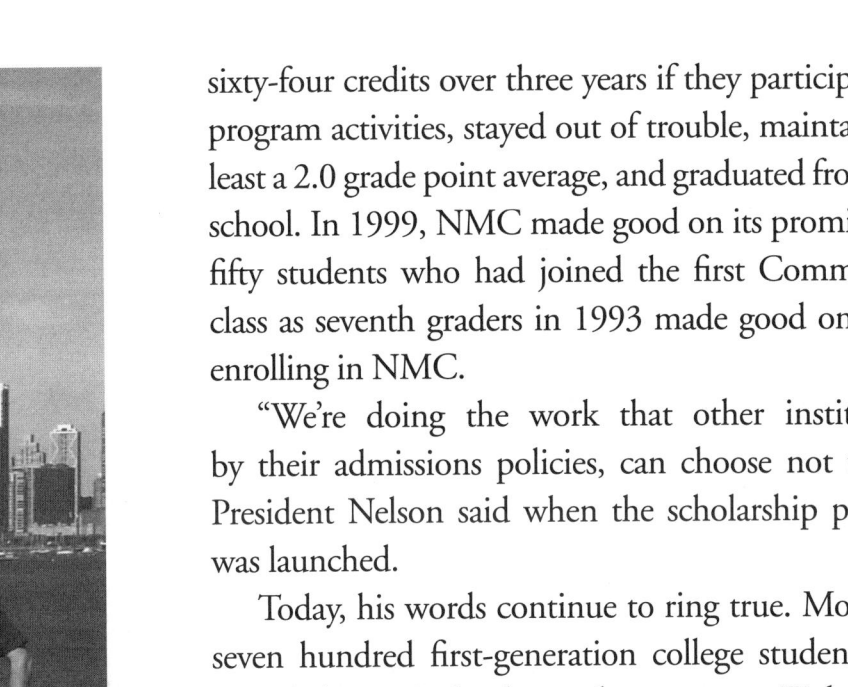

sixty-four credits over three years if they participated in program activities, stayed out of trouble, maintained at least a 2.0 grade point average, and graduated from high school. In 1999, NMC made good on its promise, and fifty students who had joined the first Commitment class as seventh graders in 1993 made good on theirs, enrolling in NMC.

"We're doing the work that other institutions, by their admissions policies, can choose not to do," President Nelson said when the scholarship program was launched.

Today, his words continue to ring true. More than seven hundred first-generation college students have attended NMC thanks to the program. Eighty-eight percent of participating students have successfully completed the program, and 80 percent of those have attended college. The Commitment Scholarship Program is funded by individual donations to the NMC Foundation, which manages an endowment that funds the annual scholarships.

Brothers Gerald Oleson, Jr. and Donald Oleson after Oleson family recognition at the 50th anniversary of the NMC BBQ, 2006.

NMC Barbecue

DESPITE GROWING INTO the biggest-known buffalo burger grill-fest anywhere, NMC's annual barbecue is about much more than a delicious lunch. Held every May on the Sunday before Memorial Day, the annual barbecue has come to epitomize the relationship between the college and the surrounding community. For organizers, volunteers, donors, students, staff, faculty, and attendees, it has become an annual tradition to share campus innovations, breaking news, national accomplishments, and fun community activities via a great big picnic.

For their years of service in donating the food for the event, in 2007 brothers Donald W. Oleson and Gerald E. Oleson Jr. received NMC's highest honor, the NMC Fellow. NMC has named fellows since 1964 as a way of recognizing and thanking those who have made special contributions to the college, whether through creative counsel, monetary resources, or inspiring leadership. The Oleson brothers have carried on the NMC barbecue tradition that was started in 1956 by their parents, Gerald and Frances Oleson. Now retired, the Oleson brothers have inspired their children to become the third generation of Olesons to continue their family's proud tradition.

Every year something new is added to the barbecue, whether it's an exhibit, an activity, or a new initiative. For example, in 2004, visual communications instructor Caroline Schaefer-Hills volunteered the services of her graphic design students to barbecue organizers. A team of five students developed promotional strategies and new logos to advertise the barbecue. Their effort worked to spread the word, and despite pouring rain, more than 6,543 meals were served. In 2007, attendees could visit the museum free, browse a used-book sale at the library, marvel over a live "buffalo cam," and tour an orchid society display.

In 2008, a very popular tradition began that continued for five years, raffling off a NMC tuition scholarship valid for ten years.

In 2009, barbecue organizers tested out the idea of composting and recycling as much of the waste generated by the event as possible and managed to cut the event's landfill waste in half.

In 2010, organizers aimed to cut down the amount of waste that went to the landfill even further, this time to zero.

Compostable plates, cups, and forks were used instead of plastic or Styrofoam, and all compostable materials, including food waste, was delivered to a commercial compost operation in Benzie County. The board of trustees dedicated additional funds to cover the higher cost of compostable materials, and more volunteers were on site to help diners dispose of their items. The effort recycled more than two thousand pounds of cardboard, forty pounds of coffee grounds, and three hundred pounds of beverage containers.

In its fifty-seven-year history, the NMC barbecue has raised more than $1.5 million for campus projects, including chairs for Milliken Auditorium, a circulatory system model that anatomy and physiology students could check out of the Osterlin Library, and technology for students' classroom use such as high-tech calculators and computer software.

Funding has been made available to highlight faculty and staff projects. The projects funded will relate to learning and benefit the community.

Cadillac Campus Closes

ALTHOUGH THE STORY of NMC's third twenty years is dominated by growth, new degree programs, new construction, and cultural advancement, there was a notable ending during this time, too. The college's Cadillac campus, opened with excitement and hope in 1987, closed at the end of the summer term in 2004.

NMC's Cadillac roots began when another community college, Kirtland, withdrew its classes there and asked whether NMC would be interested in stepping in. With "a good deal of enthusiasm and investment," NMC accepted the challenge and offered thirty-four classes to three hundred students in Cadillac in the fall of 1987.

Classes were held in the sprawling Naval Reserve building on Chestnut Street. It wasn't the same kind of environment NMC's main campus offered, but Cadillac residents and those from the surrounding area didn't have to face an hour-long commute on northern Michigan's notoriously icy two-lane roads. The goal was to have enrollment grow to seven hundred students, to work with the public schools, to assist the Cadillac community with economic development, and to establish a Small Business Assistance Center in the area.

Those ideals were never realized. By 1989, enrollment increased to 444 students, but by 1999 there were only 218 students, a number that continued to decline in 2000, 2001, and 2002. In 2000 a possible merger of NMC's Cadillac campus with those operated by Ferris State University and Davenport University was discussed but ultimately scuttled. Closing NMC's Cadillac campus was publicly considered in the spring of 2003, much to the disappointment of the Cadillac students.

By December of 2003, the campus posted a $42,000 loss for the year, enrollment had declined to just 164 students, there was a cut in NMC's state funding for the third year in a row, and Wexford County voters declined to offer any financial support. Future losses were expected, and at President Nelson's suggestion, the board of trustees voted in December of 2003 to close the Cadillac campus.

The Millages

NMC'S THIRD TWENTY YEARS began just after the college faced down the first millage failure in its history. In May of 1990, voters rejected a request for 3.0 mills. Then in 1994, the college was dealt a second financial blow when Grand Traverse County voters again approved 1.5 replacement mills but a four-county millage request that would have supplied funding to NMC from outside its home county failed.

"That was a low point," said Trustee Cheryl Gore Follette, "even though the reality is people from those areas do attend the college in large numbers and I think the idea still has validity. The challenge is to encourage people to continue to invest in education."

The college's economic experience now mirrored the nation's during the early 1990s. Budgets grew increasingly tight, and every dollar was scrutinized more carefully than ever.

Though the failure of two millages in four years was daunting, those failures laid the groundwork for the community support and solid financial footing that were to come. First, though, the college needed to find out why voters had decided the funding issue the way that they did. The best way to do that was simply to ask them.

And so, in order to be more in tune with voters' sentiments, the millage outcome led NMC to conduct its first public opinion survey. The results proved valuable enough that the college began asking people what they thought more often. As a direct result of those two millage failures, NMC now regularly polls students, alumni, and area residents on virtually every college issue.

Pin worn by supporters of the successful millage campaign of 1995.

When the college sought a millage in perpetuity in 1995, staff used voter survey responses to help craft the campaign slogan. "NMC Is Important to Me" was featured in a series of testimonial ads. The campaign was a successful one this time, with voters now firmly on the side of funding the college. Despite blizzardlike conditions on Election Day, President Tim Quinn and others spent hours standing on the corner of Division and Front streets, holding up signs urging passing motorists to vote.

The winter weather didn't keep voters home. They approved the 1.5 mill request on February 7, 1995, by a solid 62 percent.

"There's always been something very special about NMC and the pride that the community has in NMC, through all times, good and not so good," said Elaine Wood. "Over all these decades, we've been able to keep that feeling, that trust. It comes across in everything we do, from the classroom all the way through to every decision and event. That millage was a renewal of that pride."

Bond campaign workers gather in West Hall in 1999 to celebrate the win.

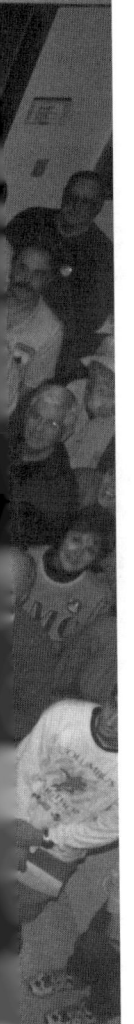

The 1999 Bond Issue

PRIOR TO THE 1990 VOTE, the idea that an NMC millage might not pass was all but inconceivable. Up until then, the college had enjoyed a forty-year track record of voter support, and so the failures in 1990 and 1994 hurt but also caused some much-needed soul searching that eventually vastly improved college-voter relations, leading to the 1995 success. By 1999, NMC's physical environment was in need of such substantial improvements, maintenance, and repairs that a bond sale was planned to finance the extensive work. It was time, once again, to ask voters for their support. The ambitious construction project would help the community for years to come, and that message needed to be communicated effectively if the project was going to be funded.

According to President Ilse Burke (1995–2000), NMC's aging infrastructure and construction needs meant that the college could have easily spent $60 million or more, but a newer survey of Grand Traverse County's likely voters showed that any request for voter funding would have to be kept lean. The college pared down its long list of potential projects, used data from the survey to draft the wording of the bond proposal it put before voters in 1999, and got busy with educating voters.

The slogan for the bond campaign was "Building a Stronger Community," and college officials were thorough this time in their efforts to disseminate it. There were advertisements on TV, on the radio, and in newspapers. There was a letters-to-the-editor campaign waged by supporters, phone banks were staffed with volunteers, and detailed mailings went out to voters.

NMC was rewarded for its frugal budgeting and good communication. On November 2, 1999, the bond passed with 54 percent approval. NMC had $34.7 million in renovation funding to work with. With this yes vote, the support of the northern Michigan community had returned in full, and the transformation of the college began.

"It was exciting to see all our facilities being upgraded," said Elaine Wood, who chaired the board of trustees' Building and Site Committee. "It gave us a renewed energy. It was a big turning point for NMC in terms of the quality of its facilities, obviously, but it also put a whole new face on our degree programs and encouraged more people to take advantage of them. It happened at a time when the region really needed them."

The white freezer building on Front Street was demolished, the maintenance department and automotive programs it housed were relocated, the library was renovated, science labs and classrooms were upgraded, state funding that had been received the previous January from the Michigan Jobs Commission for the Parsons-Stulen Technical Education Center was matched, and the technical center became the centerpiece of NMC's new Aero Park Campus. Finally, parking and traffic on the main campus were improved, and an expansion of the University Center was planned.

The college as it stands today is largely a result of the community support that began in 1951, continued through the 1980s, had a brief lag in the mid-1990s, but came roaring to life again in 1999, with the crucial passage of the infrastructure bond. The projects that the bond issue funded were completed by 2004, and that money was leveraged with federal, state, and private dollars to provide a $66 million total investment in NMC facilities by 2005. This positioned the college's physical environment—its buildings, sidewalks, and signage, for example—perfectly for the future. But the yes vote on the bond issue helped build another equally important structure more etherial in nature but no less crucial to the college's success: community support.

Economic Impact Study

FOR ALL OF NMC'S PAST SIXTY YEARS, and certainly even more so in the past twenty, anecdotal evidence has identified the college as a positive economic force in the region.

Conventional wisdom says that because of a better-educated population, northern Michigan has been able to diversify its employment beyond tourism and services. An NMC education has also helped increase innumerable local paychecks by providing new training and skills to area workers. Plus, the college itself is a major employer, annually among the top ten in Traverse City, according to the local chamber of commerce. And the college's employees certainly put at least some of their paychecks right back into the local economy.

So, no one can dispute the fact that the Grand Traverse

region has benefitted tremendously from the presence of NMC, but those benefits have always been difficult to quantify.

"Can you imagine Traverse City without Northwestern Michigan College? That's a question I ask a lot," said Trustee Gore Follette.

Then, in 2006, NMC commissioned a study specifically to put a dollar figure on everything NMC adds to the northwestern Michigan community. The results were attention-getting, to say the least.

According to the study by CCbenefits Inc., the regional economy receives $371.6 million in income due to NMC. The state of Michigan saves $1.5 million a year through improved health of its NMC students, their reduced unemployment, and the reduced likelihood that they will commit a crime. The study also found that for every $1 a student invests in an NMC education, they'll reap a $3.50 return in higher future earnings. Compared to someone with only a high school diploma, the typical associate's degree graduate from NMC will enjoy an average of $9,700 in higher earnings annually, or a whopping $372,800 over his or her working lifetime.

"NMC is a sound investment from multiple perspectives," the authors of the study concluded. "The college enriches the lives of students and increases their lifetime incomes. It benefits taxpayers by generating increased tax revenues from an enlarged economy and reducing the demand for taxpayer-supported social services. Finally, it contributes to the vitality of both the local and state economies."

At last, NMC had numbers, dollar figures, and data to back up all that anecdotal evidence. Still, as impressive as those numbers were, President Nelson stressed that there was still another number that would always be the most important one at NMC. The number one. "To me, [that] is the most important number. One. NMC makes its impact one learner at a time."

Librarian Stephanie Davis teaching (2011) in the Library Instruction Lab built in 2004 with bond renovation funds.

SOFTWARE AND HARDWARE

Staying ahead of the Curve

Northwestern
Michigan
College

Rochelle Hammontree at the remodeled Library Service Desk, 2008.

A Fiber-Optic Backbone

As the college made plans to grow in physical size throughout the early 1990s, NMC's leadership knew that growth would mean increased building needs but increased technology needs, too. When a college grows, its communication needs are sure to follow. And soon. Since 1991, those communication needs have been synonymous with computer software, hardware, and technology needs.

Those enrolled in courses on the main campus, as well as faculty and staff, would have to be able to communicate quickly and clearly with those at the University Center, the Parsons-Stulen Technical Center, the observatory, and any future NMC campuses.

In 1993, the Board of Trustees approved funding for installation of a state-of-the-art fiber-optic cable that would connect remote campus locations with facilities on the main campus.

The NMC Website

In 1996, NMC launched its Front Door Project to improve the entryway to the main campus. Front Street was realigned, the new winding entrance took drivers through a wooded canopy, and by 2000, two signs crafted out of the same stone as that used for the Dennos Museum Center were installed.

The Front Door Project was a success, essentially laying out a new welcome mat for anyone interested in NMC. However, by 2008, it was the college's virtual doorway that needed a redesign.

With prospective students as well as alumni, faculty, staff, and donors all increasingly using the internet, NMC needed to continue to present itself as as both technologically aware and up to date. It was time for the website to receive an overhaul, to keep up with the growing college.

NMC's public relations staff and Flight Path Creative, a Traverse City marketing and communications firm, spent a year working to make the college's online home one with multiple doorways, allowing the college's wide range of online visitors easy access to all the information they needed.

The overhauled website, www.nmc.edu, went live in 2009. Among the new features were easy-to-find login links, search capabilities, contact info, an A–Z index at the top of every page, better course descriptions with more details, regularly updated content, user-friendly calendars, and even high-quality video, all presented within a standardized, visually pleasing design.

Online Classes and Registration

In 2000, NMC became the first community college in Michigan to offer online registration. No longer did students have to drive to campus, wait in a long line, and fill out their paperwork by hand in order to enroll in college. With the new online registration option, they could do all this from the comfort of their homes, any time of day or night, in any kind of weather.

Students who wanted to register in person could still do so, and students who wanted to register online but didn't have access to a computer could use one for free in the library, at the bookstore, or in the registration office. There were even student volunteers ready to help any new users complete their online registration.

This technological advance was immediately popular with NMC students; it was a logical innovation after more than a decade of steadily rising enrollment and a growing array of digital learning opportunities.

Online learning debuted at the college in 1998, and within a year there were more than three hundred students enrolled in seventeen online classes. By the 2001–2002 school year, the number of online courses had increased to nearly three dozen. In those five years, from 1998 to 2002, NMC's leadership learned that online learning offered many benefits. These included expanded access, scheduling flexibility, fewer capacity constraints, a savings

Osterlin Library service desk and computer pods just prior to the remodeling done in 2004.

in travel time and cost, as well as the chance to experiment with learning opportunities in emerging areas of study.

Online courses required students to receive and submit assignments, as well as interact with their instructor and fellow students, digitally, through chat rooms, threaded discussions, and email.

The rise in enrollment numbers in NMC's online courses has shown that this method does work for many students. In the 1999 school year, NMC offered twenty-two online courses and hosted three hundred sixty-six students. Ten years later, the college offered forty-three online courses and hosted nine hundred students. In 2011, that number had grown yet again to seventy-seven courses and more than one thousand students.

After fifteen years of offering online learning options, instructors have found that the biggest challenge to digital learning remains the completion rate. Technical skills aren't a hindrance for most students the way they were for many back in 1998, when most people were not as familiar with computers and the Internet. Today, the challenge of online learning is more likely to be a lack of motivation and/or self-discipline.

Nationally, as many as half of the students enrolled in online college courses drop out. At NMC, the rate is much lower—only about 20–30 percent or less—partly because of the variety of assistance and training the college offers its online students.

Even in our tech-savvy age, this type of learning is still a new experience for many students, and so at NMC all online programs offer a short "how-to" orientation for beginners as well as a questionnaire, "Are You Ready for Online Learning?" to help prospective students determine whether digital classes are best for them.

For many students, the benefits of online learning far outweigh the challenges, and online classes often fill up first. Back in 1998, when online courses were first debuted, NMC students were not the only ones who had to "learn how to learn" when it came to online coursework. So did the instructors, many of whom had taught only in a physical classroom environment.

In order to make sure that the instructors were well versed in the technology needed to teach in a digital environment, they received and continue to receive support from three sources: a distance education team, a media resources team, and an instructional design and technology center.

There have been advances, but online learning still isn't and probably won't ever be the solution for every student. Those who are most successful—students but instructors, too—are self-directed, able to manage their time well, and computer savvy. When all is said and done, online learning does further the mission of the college: to help all learners learn.

Training Ship State of Michigan docked in harbor at the Great Lakes Campus, Maritime Academy, 2009

OF COMETS, VESSELS, AND ONLINE STREAMING

Blazing New Trails

Northwestern
Michigan
College

Comet Hyakutake *photo taken by Jerry Dobek, NMC Observatory, 1996.*

Rogers Observatory

TWO EVENTS of celestial significance took place in 2003: Mars made its closest approach to Earth in fifty thousand years and a record crowd showed up at Rogers Observatory to view the red planet. Both of these events would have thrilled the observatory's namesake, Joseph H. Rogers, who died in 1997.

Those who knew him say Rogers, an NMC science and math instructor, would certainly have appreciated all that the observatory has accomplished in the past several years. Project ASTRO, funded by the National Science Foundation in 1993 and still going strong, guides K–12 students and their families through hands-on science projects, bringing hundreds of new visitors to the observatory every month.

Finding high ground suitable for skygazing isn't such an easy task when you live in an area of lakes, rivers, and wetlands. Rogers Observatory, which contains a dome, a telescope, and a darkroom, was

Local resident and astronaut Jerry Linenger with an NMC pennant he took into outer space in 1997.

built in 1981 on a steep hilltop several miles south of the main campus and takes good advantage of the rural area's dark skies.

In 1996, when the comet Hyakutake passed Earth, a photo snapped at the observatory was later cataloged in NASA's archives as the official photo of the comet. That same year, however, NMC's frequent stargazers noticed that despite its once-remote location, light from the growing city was beginning to encroach on viewing.

And so, in 1997, the NMC observatory sparked a "dark skies initiative" so that even fifteen years after its site selection, people would still be able to see all that sparkled and orbited up in the night sky. When Comet Hale-Bopp cruised past in the spring of 1998, the Board of Trustees gathered at the observatory and viewed the comet in all its short-lived glory.

Perhaps most exciting of all for Rogers Observatory, a new high-powered computerized telescope originally earmarked for use by NASA was installed at the observatory in 2010. Thanks to the work of Rogers' protégé, NMC science instructor and observatory Director Jerry Dobek, astronomy students, members of the NMC Astronomy Club, and visitors from the community have access to the heavens via a state-of-the-art telescope.

An acquaintance of Dobek's bought the telescope from NASA at considerable expense and sold it to NMC at a discount. Dobek arranged for private donations to cover the entire cost, and now area stargazers have a sharper and more penetrating view of the changing night sky.

The Maritime Academy's Ship Comes In

WHAT'S 224 FEET LONG, 49 FEET TALL, displaces more than twenty-two hundred liquid tons, once tracked Soviet submarines and hunted drug smugglers, and has a new home in Traverse City's harbor? The Maritime Academy's biggest floating classroom.

The Stalwart-class T-AGOS *State of Michigan* was built in 1985 to spy on sonar communications from Soviet submarines. But after the end of the Cold War, the ship was transferred to the U.S. Coast Guard and retooled for its second career: heading off drug smugglers prowling the U.S. coastline. As it turned out, that work was more successfully performed by smaller, quicker vessels, so with the U.S. Maritime Administration's blessing, *State of Michigan* was reassigned in 2002 to be a teaching vessel at NMC's Great Lakes Maritime Academy (GLMA).

In August 2002, GLMA staff and graduates sailed the ship from New York City to Traverse City. Then the ship was formally christened at the Great Lakes Maritime Academy dock, preparing it for its new role as a teaching vessel. GLMA Superintendent John Tanner welcomed guests to the ceremony, Dr. Homer Nye of First Presbyterian Church of Traverse City offered an invocation, and the *State of Michigan* was transferred to its new home, NMC's maritime dock.

"This is a major leap forward in the quality of education we can provide for our students," Tanner said.

In 2003, the west wing of NMC's Great Lakes Campus opened, and the Academy, at NMC since 1969, moved into its new campus. Future plans call for the harbor to be renovated and expanded in a joint project between NMC and the U.S. Army Corps of Engineers, better accommodating the *State of Michigan*. Today, the stern of the ship is just 150 feet from the Great Lakes Campus, making it a true floating classroom.

WNMC Reaches New Audiences

"SMALL-TOWN STATION, world-class radio." From its humble beginnings broadcasting music to the college's dorms back in 1967, through its ten-watt FM debut in 1979, to the six hundred watts of power and six-county reach the station enjoys today, WNMC has earned this motto in stages.

The all-volunteer station now reaches a potential audience of more than one hundred and fifty thousand in Grand Traverse, Wexford, Antrim, Leelanau, Benzie, and Charlevoix counties. Meanwhile, its online audience at www.wnmc.org is virtually unlimited. Despite the growth, WNMC still adheres to its community-minded mission: to make on-air and production opportunities available to students and the public. In the past twenty years, that mission has been accomplished in myriad ways.

WNMC's Eric Hines (right) and Ric Bedell, 2005.

In 2000, the station initiated a number of program changes, with a stronger focus placed on broadcasting jazz in the daytime hours, from 8 a.m. to 5 p.m., and the debut of a weekday "drive time" program for listeners' evening commute from 5 to 7 p.m., featuring blues and distinctly American music.

The idea, said station General Manager Eric Hines, was to "put polish on the gem" by formalizing the broadcast schedule. Prior to 2000, the station had been organized according to creative taste and not necessarily according to any regular schedule. That changed when Hines formalized the broadcast schedule in order to build listenership and make it easier for audiences to find what they wanted to hear at regular times. The creativity of the DJs and listener requests continued unabated.

In 2002, local 7&4 television news anchor Dave Walker proposed a Sunday afternoon classic jazz program to WNMC, and his "Jazz from the Tradition" began broadcasting. By 2004, Arbitron ratings showed that formalizing the schedule had indeed paid off: WNMC listeners grew from three thousand per week in the fall of 1999 to eighty-six hundred listeners per week in the fall of 2003.

Not content to just enjoy that success, Hines started thinking about how to add more programming for listeners: a morning drive time show to "bookend" the 5–7 p.m. slot for commuters. In December of 2004, WNMC launched its morning drive time show from 6 to 8 a.m. featuring discussion of local issues with Hines and his co-host, Peter Strong.

In 2005, when Hurricane Katrina displaced New Orleans disc jockey Gerard "The Gov" Rigney and he took refuge with a friend in Traverse City, WNMC made a place for his show, "The Governor's Mansion in Exile." In 2007, the station began broadcasting on a new, more reliable transmitter purchased with funds raised by the NMC Barbecue as well as a grant from the Grand Traverse Band of Ottawa and Chippewa Indians.

"Buy a Fish" symbol for Great Lakes Campus campaign.

Also new in 2007, astronomer Michael Foerster's program, "First Light," began broadcasting its unique intersection of science and news.

New programs are continually added as others move on. Dave Walker passed away in 2008. In 2011, DJ Bill Dungjen brought his popular open mic program, "The Round Up," onto the radio. Recorded every Thursday night at the Hayloft, listeners can hear the program on WNMC twice a week.

The newest opportunity for WNMC students is participation in Radio Theater, live readings of plays and works of contemporary and classic literature. As WNMC begins a new broadcast year in 2012, new tunes, old tunes, new listeners, and regulars are sure to tune in to 90.7 FM.

NMC Board of Trustees with first female chair, Shirley Okerstrom (second from right), 1994.

GOVERNANCE

Strong, Steady Leadership

Northwestern
Michigan
College

Tim Nelson's 10th anniversary celebration invitations.

The Board of Trustees Makes a Transition

In 1993, President Tim Quinn introduced initial steps toward adopting a decision-making process known as shared governance. The result was the formation of three councils: one to plan for the future, one to make policy, and one to set the annual budget. Each of these councils had representation from faculty, administrative employees, support staff, and maintenance employees. The councils' job was to make recommendations to the president, and their meetings and minutes were always available to the public.

Along with the adoption of shared governance, the structure of the Board of Trustees was revamped beginning in 1993 and into 1994. The board went on a retreat together and adopted the Carver model of governance, which assigned the board's role as one of policy maker and the faculty's and staff's role as responsible for carrying out day-to-day operations. Instead of trying to manage projects and people, the Board of Trustees began to concern themselves more with outcomes, indicators, and measures of success.

With this change in the college's decision-making process came a new sense of openness but also lingering conflict between faculty, staff, and administration. Al Shumsky, who headed the NMC Division of Communications, referenced this in the previous history *Northwestern Michigan College: The Second Twenty Years*. At the end of the 1980s through the beginning of the 1990s, faculty expressed frustration about their lack of say-so in the administration's decision-making process. There was support for shared governance but concern that it wasn't proceeding quickly enough.

"Complaints grew about lack of communication," Shumsky wrote. "Faculty complained that they often did not know things until they read them in the *Record Eagle*."

That began to change in 1994 and 1995 as shared governance was phased in and the Board of Trustees welcomed in new leadership. In NMC's first forty years, only two men had served as chairman of the Board of Trustees: Les Biederman for the college's first twenty-five years, followed by Jim Beckett for the next fourteen. But as the college grew and changed, new voices were needed to lead. In 1994, the board chairmanship was made a rotating position, and trustees could hold the position for a maximum of three years. Shirley Okerstrom became the first woman to hold the gavel.

These changes in structure and organization had increasingly positive effects. Although some faculty and staff said they created needless and unproductive bureaucracy, most supported the idea of working toward openness and transparency in decision making. Supporters also said that the new governing style made the most of what was already a cooperative spirit among faculty and staff.

"There has always been such a rich participatory spirit at the college," said Marguerite Cotto, NMC vice president for lifelong and professional learning. "That leads to shared governance somewhat logically."

A national trend toward employee ownership was spreading across business and industry in the 1990s, affecting how committees and work groups functioned in relationship to the overall enterprise. That couldn't help but spill over to community colleges, NMC included. Also, with the financial crisis of 1990 still a vivid memory, by the mid-1990s college employees were eager for opportunities to be involved in decision making.

"As resources become more precious, people feel a need to have some say in how they're being used," Cotto said.

Shared governance intensified under Ilse Burke's presidency from 1995 to 2000. The first woman to hold the office of president at NMC, she brought with her a consensus and teamwork-oriented style that was something new in the college's experience yet just what NMC needed at the time. Burke had come to NMC from Lansing Community College, where such consensus-style leadership was the norm.

A new level of transparency took hold under Burke's direction. Shared governance was out of its infancy at NMC and moving toward full adoption. During Burke's tenure at the college, input was regularly gathered from diverse sources before decisions were made. Even more important, it was recognized and accepted that those other sources—faculty, support staff, other administrators—had a legitimate perspective and vested interest in college issues. To Burke, shared governance was not lip service; it was meant to be genuine listening even though some faculty unhappiness remained.

The mechanics of shared governance were also refined in 1999, when the Planning and Budget councils were folded into one. After all, said Stephen Siciliano, vice president for educational services, it was difficult to plan not knowing the budget, and it was difficult to budget not knowing what the plans were. At the end of the decade, the new system was working well, with a significantly increased level of trust and respect between the administration and the faculty and staff.

When Timothy Nelson became president in 2001, he expanded on the idea of shared governance with his own "community leadership" metaphor. There was an ever more increasing sense of openness when it came to a shared vision for NMC's future. Nelson's goal was for faculty, administration, support staff, and students to all hold an equal stake, much as engaged citizens do in a close-knit neighborhood, with everyone sharing responsibility both for shaping goals and for living with the outcome of working toward those goals.

Sicilliano arrived at NMC in 1985, succeeding founding professor Walter Beardslee, and said he has watched shared governance grow and thrive through three presidents. He taught history and led the humanities department before becoming an administrator in 1996.

"As he moved through the twilight of his career, I think Tim Quinn felt more confidence in the positive role that shared governance could serve at the college," Siciliano said. "When Ilse Burke served, she was fully committed to empowering the councils and making the decision-making process more transparent. Tim Nelson has been committed to shared governance, too, especially when it comes to bringing different groups together. This is the way that everyone who has a stake in NMC has their say."

Tim Quinn, president 1989-1996.

A History of Great Leadership

Tim Quinn: 1989-1996

A former Wisconsin deputy state superintendent, Tim Quinn came to the college in 1988 to serve as vice president of instructional services. Just as Dr. Philip Runkel before him, Quinn was the only candidate considered for the presidency when he was given the job in 1989.

The college needed Quinn's and the board's firm hand in his first years, as NMC's financial challenges were dominating decision making. Quinn's top accomplishments during his tenure were the turnaround of the college's budget deficit following the 1990 millage defeat; the construction and opening of the Dennos Museum Center in 1991; and the planning, fundraising, and establishment of the University Center, which opened in 1995.

Quinn readily acknowledged that he became NMC's president during a turbulent time in the college's history. First, a 15 percent deficit was found in the general fund just as he took over the leadership role. At the same time, locals were clamoring for four-year educational opportunities, an expensive proposition when money was lacking for current programs. The museum had broken ground, and the community was supportive of the project, but communication between the college and the public needed improvement.

Quinn's leadership style was, he said, top-down out of necessity. It was needed to swiftly address both the financial gaps and the communications gaps. Under his leadership, the college focused on answering a very big question: "What can NMC do to better serve the community?"

As the faculty pressed their own issues, the board stressed the importance of funding a university center, and Quinn helped get the all-important financial future of the college on a more balanced footing. His new leadership style—shared governance—was adopted, and he and the board collaborated well to divide tasks and work together toward the largest and most important goals. Only through an all-out effort could they ever be accomplished.

Putting the college back in sound financial shape was a first priority, and then fundraising for the University Center began in earnest. An incredible effort garnered $6 million in just over eight months. That success proved that despite a failed millage, shared governance was working behind the scenes and the community did support NMC when the college addressed the most pressing educational needs of the community.

"The millage in perpetuity passed, the museum and the Beckett building were completed, and the college was in good financial condition again," Quinn said, reflecting upon that turbulent and yet also exciting time. "I left feeling really good about where the college was. Today, the place is everything that a community could ask for."

Ilse Burke: 1996-2001

Ilse Burke came to NMC in August of 1995 as the vice president for educational services and was named president a year later, serving immediately after Tim Quinn.

"It's more complex when you're sitting in the president's chair," she said, "because you have to balance all the needs, not just think about your own department."

Burke spent five years in that challenging role and said her most lasting accomplishment was to help develop a workable strategic plan.

"I inherited a stable financial situation, but we weren't sure where we were going," she said, shortly before leaving the post

Ilse Burke, president 1996-2001.

in 2000. "Now we have a strategic plan, but it must become a mind-set; we can't think we're done when the initiatives are completed. There's always more to do."

The $34 million bond issue was approved under her tenure, and its success propelled the strategic plan into action. Without passage of the bond, it's safe to say that the strategic plan in its ambitious entirety and all the positive growth of the college could never have been implemented.

Summing up her experience serving as president of NMC, Burke said, "It's been very enjoyable and rewarding—and also very intense in terms of energy. You can't step out of the job."

"I have always been a very participative leader," she said, adding, however, that it was the faculty and staff buy-in that made shared governance work well into her presidency. "It doesn't matter what you call it; if people don't believe you're serious about sharing some of that leadership, then you're just going through the motions, and it doesn't work," she said. "They [faculty, staff, Board of Trustees] were willing to take a chance and see if it would work."

Tim Nelson, president 2001-present.

Tim Nelson: 2001-Present

At a special meeting on January 17, 2001, the NMC Board of Trustees voted unanimously to offer the NMC presidency to Timothy Nelson. The decision came after a national search and a series of open forums with three finalists.

The board praised the "breadth and depth of experience," particularly business and educational experience, that Nelson brought to the job.

Responding to the announcement that he was NMC's new president, Nelson referenced the college's accomplishments to date. "Reading the two histories of NMC, *The First Twenty Years* and *The Second Twenty Years*," Nelson said, "I see our link with the past in our commitment to the community, to learning, and to our spirit of innovation. These must be retained and nurtured as we continue our journey."

Under Nelson's leadership, the college has done just that. The bond issue funding was managed well and leveraged with other funding to virtually transform the physical environment of the main campus. Additional funding for the Parsons-Stulen Technical Education Center first imagined under President

Burke was a sought-after coup for the community; the Dennos Museum Center continued to attract world-class exhibits, performers, and speakers; and the addition of the Great Lakes Campus was another visible accomplishment.

"From a business perspective, he's been gangbusters," said Trustee Cheryl Gore Follette.

Nelson came to NMC from Olivet College, where he served as vice president for finance and administration. Prior to his work at Olivet, Nelson worked for Great Lakes Capital Management Corporation in Milwaukee, Wisconsin, and was president and founder of Access Technologies Corporation in Houghton, Michigan. Nelson had also taught in the School of Business and Engineering Administration at Michigan Technological University in Houghton, one of his alma maters.

NMC's current president also had a few roots at NMC. Before being named president, he was NMC's executive director of administrative services. Back in 1975 he had been a residence hall supervisor. All this varied experience made Nelson just the right president for the college at just the right time.

During his tenure, NMC has seen double-digit growth in student enrollment. For example, in the fall of 2009, academic enrollment was 5,064 students, an 11 percent jump over enrollment the year before. Proof that NMC is reaching a diverse audience and not only those straight out of high school is the fact that the biggest growth has come from older students, those over age twenty-six, many of whom have come back to college for additional course work in their chosen profession or retraining in response to an economic downturn.

Since Nelson became president in 2001, NMC has also added many new degree and certificate programs, opened a new campus, and lobbied lawmakers in Lansing to allow the college to offer four-year degrees in nursing and maritime studies, culinary arts, and energy production. During all these advances, state aid has remained flat, many faculty members have opted for early retirement, and students have increasingly expected state-of-the-art facilities and access to the latest technology. Through all of this growth, change, and student expectations, under Nelson's leadership NMC has never been stronger financially.

As Nelson and the Board of Trustees lead the college toward a future that will require global interactivity, the challenge of making sure that "all learners learn" will surely grow.

"It's all about keeping learning at the center," Nelson said. "There's value in every kind of learning that takes place here. Whether for a career-related degree or for personal enrichment, we are giving our students the skills, experiences, and values they need to thrive in a truly global society."

Great Lakes Campus harbor view.

THE FOURTH TWENTY YEARS

What's Next?

Northwestern
Michigan
College

"You can learn so much from people that are from different cultures. There's so much more out there. It takes the blinders off."

Anjanette Merriweather, NMC Visual Communications student

"My first time out of state was also my first time out of the country. It really opened my eyes to the possibilities of everything."

Ashley Flees, NMC Liberal Arts student

1. NMC Freshwater Studies student trip to Costa Rica.
2. Varanasi (India): Photographs by Larry K. Snider, The Dennos Museum Center.
3. Cuadros from the Peruvian Women of Pamplona Alta, The Dennos Museum Center.
4. Wan Liya (China), Artist in Residence, The Dennos Museum Center.
5. NMC Aviation student trip to England.
6. NMC Freshwater Studies student trip to Costa Rica.
7. NMC Aviation student trip to England.
8. Golden Dragon Acrobats (China), The Dennos Museum Center.
9. Tibetan monks mandala project, The Dennos Museum Center.

Global initiative highlights, 2011.

Global Initiatives

As TECHNOLOGY, MEDIA, EASE OF TRAVEL, and population migration continue to shrink our world, higher education must adapt to serve its students as well. And so the new question NMC leaders are asking at the close of the college's first sixty years is this: How do we prepare our students to succeed in an intercultural and globalized economy?

Partial answers will be to offer NMC students a variety of intercultural learning opportunities including study abroad, cross-cultural learning teams and projects, and access to Skype and other technologies that will allow students to develop and build on valuable international relationships. In order to ensure that NMC students are prepared for success in our new global society, they need to have international opportunities.

So committed is the Board of Trustees to the idea of offering students global experiences that it has even been made part of the strategic portion of the new master plan. This is a specific identified strategic outcome: "As part of their degree programs, all learners will have intercultural learning opportunities. Learners will experience an intercultural and diverse student body at NMC."

Students of the future will benefit from what the NMC leadership is prioritizing today. Evidence of this can already be seen in the results of these first experiences.

"You can learn so much from people that are from different cultures," said Anjanette Merriweather, liberal arts student and editor of the NMC magazine. "There's so much more out there. It takes the blinders off."

These eye-opening experiences will require funding, and in celebration of NMC's sixtieth year and his own tenth anniversary leading the college, President Nelson spearheaded the Global Opportunities Fund. This fund will offer a variety of opportunities for students and faculty, including scholarships for students to attend international conferences, sign up for an internship, or volunteer in another country; funding for global experts to come to NMC and teach; funding for faculty and staff expeditions abroad; and work with area businesses to develop international internships.

NMC, Always Looking Ahead

IN 2011, THE BOARD OF TRUSTEES of NMC added to the college's strategic plan and adopted five strategic directions for the college. They were (1) ensure that NMC learners are prepared for success in a global society and economy, (2) establish national and international competencies and provide leadership in select educational areas connected to the regional economy and assets, (3) deliver learning through a networked workforce, (4) establish lifelong relationships with learners, and (5) transcribe most learning to establish credentials of value.

This is not just a piece of paper but a dynamic document, says Trustee Doug Bishop. "The greatest challenge to the college and, hence, to the board is and has been developing and implementing a viable strategic plan taking into account the continually changing funding structure for community colleges," he said. "We have been blessed in recent years by the leadership of Tim Nelson and an extremely competent staff and faculty."

Way back in 1951, NMC was the state's first comprehensive community college; however, the goal of educating northern Michigan students for a global society hadn't even occurred to the original founders. They wanted opportunities for young people so that they wouldn't have to move away from Traverse City to seek their future. Today, not only do students stay here but also they have begun to arrive from other parts of the country and even the world. NMC has recognized that even being rooted in northern Michigan requires some knowledge of the world outside the mitten.

"The more we get people to look at the future and beyond their current physical surroundings, the better equipped they are to adapt, to absorb changes, and to use the skills they learn here and elsewhere to live more productive, happier lives," said President Nelson. "We will not truly be able to serve the learners in our region without serving the world."

Our modern world now requires global interaction. NMC strives to provide international opportunities for its students, staff, and faculty.

"I see NMC getting more and more involved in international activity," said Elaine Wood. "Some people might see that as being out of sync with the role of a community college, but it really isn't at all. We live in a global world. NMC's leaders are paving the way, and we will see more and more international connections that will benefit our local businesses and our students."

Some of that international outreach is already happening. For example, aviation students have been to Great Britain, and long-standing internship programs send students to Germany and Japan. Visual communications students have gone to Europe, preengineering students have visited Russia, and water studies students have worked in Costa Rica. NMC will keep the question of when the college will become a four-year institution at the forefront. Until then, Director Aaron Cook's philosophy of aviation education at NMC has a universal message across all departments:

"We provide a high-quality program for a reasonable price, not only for people in this region, but we also attract people from around the country and even around the world. Although it's a community college, you get people from around the world who come here."

Despite the changes of the past twenty years, or perhaps even because of them, it is impossible to imagine what northern Michigan would look like—would *be* like—without the college. "People here feel a sense of ownership of NMC that is fairly unique," said Kathleen Guy.

By providing quality affordable access to higher education to students of all ages and backgrounds, NMC has woven itself indelibly into our region by appealing to a diverse community of learners. Learning has been at the center of all that NMC has achieved and will continue to be at the center of all NMC will achieve in its next twenty years and beyond.

So what *is* in store for NMC in the next twenty years? Even more innovation, technological advances, and international opportunities. "We have to find ways," said President Nelson, "to help our faculty, staff, students, and community understand there is a global dimension to everything we do."

What's equally important is the work that occurs after NMC sends a learner on his or her way out into the world. And even with a taste of life and work outside Michigan, outside the Midwest, and even outside the United States, 80 percent of the college's alumni either choose to stay in our region or, if they do move away for a time, eventually return to live, work, and serve their home community, bringing the fruits of their education home to the community where it all began.

Appendices

BOARD OF TRUSTEES

NMC is governed by a publicly elected board of trustees that serves a six-year term. Trustees at the close of the college's third twenty years, in 2011, were:

 Robert T. Brick, Chair

 William D. Myers, Vice Chair

 Douglas S. Bishop, Secretary

 Susan K. Sheldon, Treasurer

 K. Ross Childs

 Cheryl Gore Follette

 Walter J. Hooper

PRESIDENTS

Tim Quinn
Ilse Burke
Tim Nelson

IMOGENE WISE FACULTY EXCELLENCE AWARD RECIPIENTS

2011:   Dr. Blake Key
2010:   Steve Drake
2009:   Dr. Amjad Khan
2008:   Connie Jason
2007:   Dr. Keith Overbaugh
2006:   Mark Nelson
2005:   Johnathon Mauk
2004:   Michael Jacobson
2003:   Sean Ruane
2002:   Mike Surgalski
2001:   Sonja Olshove
2000:   Doug Domine
1999:   Mary Quinn
1998:   James Press
1997:   William Faulk

1996: Richard Cookman
1995: Adam Gahn
1994: Debra Pharo
1993: Martin Trapp
1992: James Coughlin
1991: John Tanner

ADJUNCT FACULTY EXCELLENCE AWARD RECIPIENTS

2011: Dr. Mark Holley
2010: Lisa Blackford
2009: Gary Sanborn
2008: Stephen Lockman
2007: Jason Teichman
2006: Karl Sporck
2005: Peter Baumeler
2004: Ted Reese
2003: Jerry Gates
2002: Jerry Dobek
2001: Regis McCord
2000: Susan Odgers
1999: Gregory LaCross

OUTSTANDING ALUMNI

2011: Ruth Ann Lamott (Class of 1965–1966)
Glen Wolff (Class of 1973)
2010: Ross Biederman (Class of 1959)
Susie Janis (Class of 1967)
2009: Verna Bartnick (1960s)
Bruce Byl (Class of 1979)
Tim Dunn (Class of 1992)
2008: Todd McMillen (Class of 1985)
2007: John Robert Williams (Class of 1976)
2006: James DeLapa (Class of 1956)
2005: Larry Inman (Class of 1974)
2004: Jean M. Rokos (Class of 1975)
2003: Jason Allen (Class of 1983)
2002: Maurie Dennis (Class of 1965)
2001: Student Government Association Presidents
2000: John Pelizzari (Class of 1975)
1999: Walter J. Hooper (Class of 1968)
1998: James Clancy (Class of 1955)
1997: Richard Benedict (Class of 1984)
1996: Lloyd V. Hackley (Class of 1964)
1993: John and Gloria Lyon (Class of 1979)

FOUNDATION EXCELLENCE AWARD WINNERS

Foundation Excellence Award recipients model NMC values in their daily work and are committed to the NMC mission by modeling the quality service principles of respect and empowerment of others. They focus on meeting the needs of students and clients, display commitment to continuous improvement, and manifest respect for teamwork.

2011
Kathleen Guy
Cathy Jarvi
Gerald Provencher
Elizabeth Stevens
Ann Swaney

2010
Alycia Rhein

Career & Employment Services Team:
Shauna Eddy
Erica Hamilton
Kristy McDonald
Bonnie Shumaker
Michael Wagner

2010 *(continued)*

Institutional Advancement Staff:
Sonia Clem
Dave Dalquist
Heather Durocher
Martha Griggs
Paul Heaton
Eric Hines
Jan Neumann
Cari Noga
Cheri Paul
Chris Studenka
Heidi Yaple
Megan Young

2009
Deb Faas
Ruth Ann LaMott

2008
William Donberg
Bronwyn Jones

2007
Karen Giddis

Scheduling Software Implementation Team:
Anna Bachman
Sue DeCamillis
Sue Gattshall
Cathy Jarvi
Deb Patterson
Lisa Krupp-Wilmeth
Dorothy Witt

2006

Sallie Donovan
Jan Root

Student Support Services/Tutorial Center Team:
Denny Everett
Michelle Poertner
Mary Ann Schneider

2005

Lucille A. House
Karen L. Kahler

Center for Learning Team:
Thomas F. Auch
Alison B. Collins
Terry A. Barr

2005 *Center for Learning Team: (continued)*
Chandler Kahler
James J. Lijewski
Daniel D. Tollefson

2004
Linda L. Rea
Bryce E. Turner

College Relations & Foundation Team:
Karen Anderson
Kathy Lievense
Teri Hedrich
Sonia Clem
Jan Neumann
Margaret Fox
Eric Hines

Human Resources Support Team:
Lori L. Hodek
Carol A. Kasper

White Pine Press Advisor Team:
Jill L. Hinds
Marilyn S. Jaquish

2003

Shirley F. Boyce
Cathleen R. Muma
James G. Press
Jenny L. Winowiecki

GLMA Faculty and Staff:
John H. Berck
Michael W. Hochscheidt
Jean H. Johnson
Robert D. Mason
Judith A. Rokos
David T. Sobolewski
Michael J. Surgalski
Jerry J. Williams

2002

Edward P. Bailey
Laura J. Carmickle
Michelle L. Ames
Dennos Museum Center Volunteers

Dennos Museum Center Staff:
Judith A. Albers
Janet E. Bay

2002 *Dennos Museum Center Staff:* (continued)
Kara M. Berg
Kathleen M. Buday
Carolyn A. Drake
Ernest S. Dunham
Kevin M. Gills
Kim H. Hanninen
Patrick A. Phelan
Christina L. Schaub
Terry L. Tarnow
Rosemary V. Tiberg
Robert S. Weiler
Peter M. Wiejaczka
Deborah M. Willson

2001

Karen J. Anderson
Karen F. Howie

2000

Upward Bound Program Staff:
Nicole Basch
Ann Dane
Scott Herzberg
Barbara Zupin

Media Services Technical Support Team:
Alan Beer
Robert Chauvin
Dennis Schultz
Jenny Winowiecki

1999

Laura Schmidt
David Terrell

Center for Learning Team:
Alison Collins
Mike Connolly
J. David Crawford
Cherie Domine
Chad Kahler
Michelle Poertner
David Hundt
Amy Middleton
Tom Auch
Cari Burke
Roberta Teahen

1998
Gary Klotzbach
Keith Overbaugh
Pat Salathiel

1997
David Dalquist
John C. Pahl
Marjory Smith

1996
Ronda M. Edwards-Barth
Marilyn S. Jaquish

1995
Michael N. Connolly
Sallie A. Donovan
Karen L. Kahler

Team Award:
Jay D. Beery
Rebecca L. Chartier
Susan L. DeCamillis
David K. Donovan
Catherine L. Jarvi
Christine M. Keenan
Ruth M. Rague

1994
John McDonald
Jim Press
Karen Sabin

1993
Debra J. Faas
Robert A. Chauvin

Team Award:
Kenneth W. Masck
Michael A. McIntosh
Donald L. Thompson